*In her book, **TECHNOGEDDON:** ʾ
effectively lays out the ominous
planet. Her book reveals how Trans~~humanism, Robotics,~~
the resulting hellish hybridization of humans could soon cast us into spurious enslavement
and death. Find out what every Believer needs to know in the twilight of human history.*

~ ***Steve Quayle***, Author of Terminated, Xenogenesis and Genetic Armageddon

TECHNO-GEDDON

The Coming Human Extinction

SHEILA ZILINSKY

Cover design and interior formatting by:
King's Custom Covers
www.KingsCustomCovers.com

Copyright 2021 by KINGSMEN Publishing and Sheila Zilinsky. All rights reserved. Except for use in a review, no portion of this book may be reproduced in any form without the express written permission of the publisher.

For more information please contact Sheila Zilinsky Ministries at:
www.sheilazilinsky.com/contact

ISBN: 979-8525052765

First Edition: July 2021

10 9 8 7 6 5 4 3 2 1

ACKNOWLEDGMENTS

I would like to give a special thank you
to the following people, without whom I could not have
accomplished this book...

Steve Quayle

Dr. Michael Lake

Dr. Tom Horn and Skywatch TV

Dr. Daniel Morano

Judi Klug

Darrin Geisinger

Carter Zilinsky

FOREWORD
by Dr. Michael Lake

In the Twenty-First Century, the Church will face spiritual warfare on an unprecedented scale. As Watcher-enhanced technologies and advancements proliferate within the darkest corners of humanity, we will face the perils of techno-sorceries never imagined by the early Church. From the ability to cast magic spells through subspace via scalar waves targeting DNA, to new mind-control techniques delivered through everyday electronic devices, the armies of the Son of Perdition are assembling their weaponry for their end-time assault.

However, Jesus foresaw these days during His ministry on Earth. He assembled His disciples at Ground Zero of the Watcher Invasion, Mount Hermon. It was at this strategic place that He looked beyond the Early Church to see our day and proclaimed:

> *"And I say also unto thee, That thou art Peter, and upon this rock I will build my church; and the gates of hell shall not prevail against it. And I will give unto thee the keys of the kingdom of heaven: and whatsoever thou shalt bind on earth shall be bound in heaven: and whatsoever thou shalt loose on earth shall be loosed in heaven." Matthew 16:18-19*

Biblically, the gates of the city represent the full leadership of that city. Here in Matthew, Jesus was referring to the full leadership and council of Hell itself. During the time of the Early Church, the primary leadership of the Watchers were bound, and not released until around the turn of the Twentieth Century. In other words, Jesus saw our day and knew that the Holy Spirit would release the knowledge and prayers that we needed to overcome their machinations.

My good friend, Sheila Zilinsky, is a prayer warrior that the Holy Spirit is speaking to today. She has spent many years researching the plans of the enemy and has prayerfully sought answers to overcome their advanced tactics of warfare.

I encourage you to seriously and prayerfully read this book and allow the Holy Spirit to show you the things that you need to address in your own life and prophetic ways to assault the gates of Hell to win the souls of humanity to Christ.

> ~ *Dr. Michael K. Lake,*
> *Author of The Shinar Directive*
> *and The Sheeriyth Imperative*

Table of Contents

Introduction 1

Chapter 1: Original DNA Tampering 5

Chapter 2: Days of Noah 2.0 — Mutagenic Monsters ... 13

Chapter 3: H+ — Transhumanism 33

Chapter 4: AI — Antichrist's Intelligence 45

Chapter 5: Beast-Tech 61

Chapter 6: Robo-Tech — Rise of the Machines 69

Chapter 7: Fallen Angel-Tech – Tower of Babel & Techno-Sorcery 89

Chapter 8: Alien-Tech — The Nazis, UFOs & The Occult Connection 109

Chapter 9: Covid, Demon-Tech & The God Code 121

Chapter 10: Technolon Rising: The Last Stand 137

Afterword 148

Appendix 1: Warfare Prayer Against Techno-Sorcery, Digital Dictatorship and Human Extinction 151

Introduction

Humanity stands on the brink of a technological revolution that will radically alter the way we live, work, and relate to one another. In its scale, scope, and complexity, the transformation will be unlike anything mankind has experienced.

One thing is remarkably clear, the science of achieving God-like immortality has never been more advanced. The war to vanquish God's creation of mankind has been brewing for thousands of years and it's coming to a head. The Bible says that Lucifer (Satan) was cast down from heaven when he attempted mutiny because he wanted to be "like the Most High." Jesus told us he comes only to "steal, kill and destroy." For thousands of years the enemy's plan has been not only to usurp God's authority, but also to wipe out God's creation—those made in His likeness and image. Satan was the purveyor of the very first lie on earth. He peddled the deceit to the very first humans in the Garden when he convinced Adam and Eve that God lied.

> *The serpent was more crafty than any of the wild animals that God had made. He said to the woman, Did God really say You must not eat from any tree in the garden? The woman said to the serpent, we may eat fruit from the trees in the garden, but God did say, you must not eat fruit from the tree that is in the middle of the garden, and you must not touch it, or you will die. You will not certainly die, the serpent said to the woman. For God knows that when you eat from it your eyes will be opened, and you will be like God. Genesis 3:1-4 (NIV)*

The lie was this: by breaking one of God's laws they could become god-like.

Why does becoming god-like appeal to us somewhere intrinsically, deep inside us, capturing our will and causing us to stumble time and again? It's called rebellion, and Satan truly was the original rebel.

Fast-forward to today. This time Satan comes to us with his lies not as a serpent, but rather in the name of science, making beguiling promises. This notion that advancements in technology can "improve" the human condition is couched in seductive metaphors and alluring assurances of making people "enhanced" versions of themselves. You, as a regular man or woman, are inferior in your current form. The way God created you is "second rate" and "outdated." You are in bad need of an upgrade, and unless you want to get left behind you need to act. Otherwise, you will always be a substandard citizen. After all, who wants to be below par?

The lie being touted today is a glorious future of eternal life. It's a terribly effective lie, and like Satan's first promise to Eve, people are still falling for it, thousands of years later, even if it costs them their very souls. The Bible tells us that God's People are destroyed through a lack of knowledge. This book's aim is to open the eyes of those who are oblivious to this diabolical and very deadly agenda. It is to sound the proverbial alarm so that we can head off what is poised to be, literally, the extinction of humanity.

In the following chapters, I will lay out how we are being systematically misled and brainwashed to embrace a plethora of terrifying technological ideas, malevolent advancements and horrifying practices that are modifying us in ways that could ultimately cause our demise. I will show you how a sinister cabal has concocted a diabolical endgame. I will further illustrate how the frightening scenario being assembled before our very eyes is clearly foretold in God's Holy Word. The Bible lays out what will happen during a final push by these evil forces in an effort to destroy good. We are at a very important moment in history, marching toward an unknown destination for humanity's very future. It doesn't take a rocket scientist or a Bible scholar to see the repercussions of tampering with genomes, editing DNA, and creating Artificial Intelligence (AI) atrocities that are thrusting us back to the days of Noah, threatening our very existence. This holocaust is fast approaching and if not thwarted, the disastrous implications for all people on earth could be irrevocable.

The good news is that there is still time to stop this attack on our planet. The key is to make enough people aware of the danger so that something can be done. People are resourceful and resilient. When they become aware of perils, they often devise amazing ways to head off the disasters.

The truth makes us free but we first must learn what the truth really is. Only then can we see the path that leads to freedom.

Ephesians 5:11 warns that we are to have nothing to do with evil agendas, but rather expose (reprove) them. I believe most people would agree that if life itself is in danger we should all strive to stand up against this agenda. The bottom line is that mankind sits at the brink of its own demise, *racing to the point of extinction…*

CHAPTER 1
ORIGINAL DNA TAMPERING

"And whereas you saw iron mixed with miry clay, they shall mingle themselves with the seed of men." ~Daniel 2:43

Many Bible scholars believe Genesis 6 points to a world-changing event prior to the Great Flood (deluge). The catastrophic destruction of men and animals by an overwhelming flood in the days of Noah (some estimate 2370 B.C.E.) is said to be the greatest cataclysm in all of human history.

The flood was sent by God because the earth became filled with wickedness, violence and genetic corruption. The apocryphal Book of Enoch seems to fill in some details of the Genesis 6 account, saying that a group of angelic beings called Watchers descended to the summit of Mount Hermon in the days of the patriarch Jared to "mate with the daughters of men."

> *There were giants in the earth in those days; and also after that, when the sons of God came in unto the daughters of men, and they bare children to them, the same became mighty men which were of old, men of renown. Genesis 6:4*
>
> *And when the sons of men had multiplied, in those days, beautiful and comely daughters were born to them. And the*

> *Watchers, sons of heaven, saw them and desired them. And they said to one another, Come, let us choose for ourselves from the daughters of men, and let us beget for ourselves children…And they descended onto the peak of Mount Hermon. 1 Enoch 6*

The *Days of Noah* was a period of time when the Nephilim first appeared, a time of rampant immorality, tremendous violence, and unchecked genetic corruption/mutation. A group of Fallen Angels traded their angelic legacy for a bestial existence. They produced offspring, a hybrid race of part celestial and part human entities. Often called giants, when their human part died their celestial part became disembodied spirits, continuing to do the work of destruction until the day of Judgment.

The word in the original Hebrew is related to the verb *naphal*, meaning "to fall." The Hebrew word *Nephilim* means "fallen ones." Nephilim is a plural word, meaning that there is more than one. It is significant to note that the word Nephilim is used only two times in the Bible, once in Genesis 6:4 and once in Numbers 13:30-33, both times translated as "giants" in the King James Version. It was the fallen ones, the Nephilim, that genetically corrupted the hereditary line in human beings, and did so both before and after the Great Flood of Noah's day.

As soon as the angels rebelled against God and descended to earth, they lost their transcendental qualities, and were invested with sublunary bodies, so that a union with the daughters of men became possible.

God-men, entities, and demigods, such as Apollo, Baal, Beelzebub, Belial, Chemosh, Dagon, Gilgamesh, Moloch, Nimrod, Osiris, etc. are named after Fallen Angels. But more on this in later chapters.

"Azazel taught men how to make slaughtering knives, arms, shields, and coats of mail. He showed them metals and how to work them, and armlets and all sorts of trinkets, and the use of rouge for the eyes, and how to beautify the eyelids, and how to ornament themselves with the rarest and most precious jewels and all sorts of paints.

"The chief fallen angel, Shemhazai, instructed them in exorcisms and how to cut roots;

Armaros taught them how to raise spells;

Barakel, divination from the stars;

Kawkabel, astrology;

Ezekeel, augury from the clouds;

Arakiel, the signs of the earth;

Samsaweel, the signs of the sun;

Seriel, the signs of the moon.

"The blood spilled by the giants cried out unto heaven from the ground, and four archangels accused the fallen angels and their sons before God, whereupon He gave the following orders to them:

"Uriel was sent to Noah to announce to him that the earth would be destroyed by a flood, and how to save his own life.

"Raphael was told to put the fallen angel Azazel into chains, cast him into a pit of sharp and pointed stones in the desert Dudael (the Cauldron of God) and cover him with darkness, and so he was to remain until the great day of judgment.

"Gabriel was charged to proceed against the bastards and reprobate, the sons of the angels begotten with the daughters of men, and plunge them into deadly conflict with one another.

"Michael handled Shemhazai's ilk who first caused them to witness the death of their children in their bloody combat

> *with each other, and then he bound them and pinned them under the hills of the earth, where they will remain for seventy generations, until the day of judgment, to be carried thence to the fiery pit of hell." ~Legends of the Jews, Volume 1*

Essentially, these Fallen Angels gave mankind dark occult powers, advanced sciences and technologies. You could call it *Fallen Angel tech (the knowledge of good and evil)*, but more on that later…

Much confusion has arisen over the terms "Fallen Angels," "giants," "Nephilim," and "demons." The Bible, however, draws clear distinctions.

Fallen Angels came to earth in their rebellion against God. Jude 1:6 states:

> *"And the angels which kept not their first estate, but left their own habitation, he hath reserved in everlasting chains under darkness unto the judgment of the great day."*

In other words, these Fallen Angels left their own habitation, their *first estate*. They didn't stay in the heavenly realm or plane of existence created for them by God. Instead, they came to earth and had sex with human women. From those unsanctioned sexual unions, the giants were born, subsequently to become the basis of all worldwide myths and legends about the "mighty men of renown," the god-men.

There's another "As in the days of Noah" connection to today that we are now seeing play out. We return to Genesis 6:4.

> *"The Nephilim [giants] were on the earth in those days, and also afterward, when the sons of God came in to the daughters of men, and they bore children to them. Those were the mighty men who were of old, men of renown."*

In the last part of this verse, most English translations use the phrase *mighty men* as a synonym for the giants. It is translated as mighty men rather than giants because the word in this passage for "men" is *enowsh* which literally means "men." This makes sense because these creations are part men and part angel.

While the word Nephilim is only used twice within the Old Testament, giants are referred to as the Rephaim over 20 times in the Old Testament. They even have a specific valley named after them known as the *Valley of the Rephaim*, as described in the Book of Joshua. It's clear that the word Rephaim is a very specific reference to the giants born of the union between Fallen Angels and the women. The resulting hybrid progeny possessed supernatural strength and size, and often exhibited cannibalism.

Fallen Angels can transform themselves (and likely will continue to do this) into physical forms with all the appropriate sexual functions and reproductive capabilities that God created for mankind. This doesn't happen in heaven, but it does on Earth with Fallen Angels.

There is also significant confusion regarding the descriptive term *demon* and the entities the term represents. The terms Nephilim or Rephaim are often mistakenly used to describe demons, or are called demons. This is incorrect.

A demon is a disembodied spirit (*daimon*). It arises when a hybrid (part angel, part human) dies. Angels don't die, but Adam saw to it that humans do. So when the human part of these hybrid entities died/was killed, the angelic/spiritual part became disembodied spirits. Their evil appetites and cravings did not change. They still want sexual contact and crave human flesh. And so, to satisfy these passions and lusts, demons seek to possess and afflict living beings, using them as vessels to partake of their previous embodied existence. Thus, demons are evil spirits.

I mentioned earlier that the Fallen Angels possessed advanced knowledge. The knowledge of good and evil. This included science, technology, alchemy, sorcery, metallurgy, mathematics, cosmology and other fields. This knowledge helped man build ancient super-civilizations which many researchers now believe existed in the antediluvian world. Ancient Pre-Flood civilizations built extremely sophisticated monolithic structures and left evidence of their highly advanced technological and scientific civilization.

It is believed that these ancient races of super men/god-men, established the legendary civilizations of Atlantis, Thule, and Hyperborea, etc. The symbols found on monolithic monuments, including pictures and inscriptions, are perhaps evidence of some kind of visitors "from another world" who would one day return.

The fallen ones also disobeyed God by reproducing with various species of animals. The ancient legends of minotaurs, mermaids, elves, half-human and half-horse beings, and fish-like creatures that were both men and animal are based on this. When we study Plato's account of Atlantis, we see that he believed the philosopher kings who ruled Atlantis came from ancient beings that were part animal and part human.

The point is that the Fallen Angels had ultimately corrupted the DNA of every species on earth and all of mankind, except for Noah who was "perfect in his generations." Genesis 6:9

They broke God's "after its own kind" rule, which stated human beings should mate only with other human beings. Some of us believe that the manipulation of DNA may have had a deeper purpose—namely, to create a hybrid form that neither the spirit of man nor the spirit of God would inhabit, but was a perfect design for the Watchers to inhabit.

It could be said this way, if human DNA could be corrupted, then no Savior ("seed of the woman") would be born, Satan's head would not be "bruised," and mankind would be lost forever, giving Satan the victory over God's creation.

> *"And I will put enmity between thee and the woman, and between thy seed and her seed; it shall bruise thy head, and thou shalt bruise his heel."* Genesis 3:15

Do we see now why God ordered His people to maintain a pure bloodline and not to intermarry with the other nations? When men breached this command and the mutated DNA began rapidly spreading among humans and animals, God instructed Noah to build an ark and prepare for a flood that would destroy every living thing.

One of the key elements of the *Days of Noah* was that the genetics of the human race was under full assault. This is a very important point.

The ancient records, including those of the Bible, describe the cause of the Flood as happening in response to "all flesh having become 'corrupted', both man and beast."

> *And God said unto Noah, The end of all flesh is come before me; for the earth is filled with violence through them; and, behold, I will destroy them with the earth.* Genesis 6:13

The DNA of the Fallen Angels was passed from one generation to the next, corrupting each child born from this lineage. Thus, the human bloodline was corrupted by these Fallen Angels as well as their hybrid offspring. Worse, given their giant size, superior strength and ruthless nature, it isn't too hard to imagine that they also had an unfair advantage when competing with human men for women, for food, and eventually for existence.

The genetic line had become so corrupted that by the time of Noah, God had to destroy ALL LIFE on the planet in order to bring about the seed of the woman (Genesis 3:15). The Flood wiped out every living thing except for Noah and his family, and the specific animals which God Himself sent to the Ark.

So, he destroyed all living things which were on the face of the ground: both man and cattle, creeping thing and bird of the air. They were destroyed from the earth. Only Noah and those who were with him in the ark remained alive. And the waters prevailed on the earth one hundred and fifty days (Genesis 7:1–24).

After the Flood wiped out the corrupted DNA, God commanded Noah to *be fruitful, and multiply* (Genesis 1:28).

Why did this global catastrophic event happen?

It is my belief that the flood came because God's creation crossed a line via disobedience and rebellion. Throughout the Bible, we read about bloodlines and genetics and one theme emerges: God does NOT want us tampering with our DNA. Or our blood, for that matter. He put it in us for a reason. We are, again, made in the likeness and image of God, fearfully and wonderfully made. God put the "breath of the spirit of life" into His creation, for lack of a better word, a *life-force*, that separates us from everything else.

So what would cause a return of the Nephilim?

Perhaps it has to do with today's tampering with our genetic line and the rise of advanced technology…

CHAPTER 2
DAYS OF NOAH 2.0: MUTAGENIC MONSTERS

"Trying to read our DNA is like trying to understand software code – with only 90% of the code riddled with errors. It's very difficult in that case to understand and predict what that software code is going to do." ~Elon Musk

Throughout history, mythology has included many particularly famous hybrids, including those from Egyptian and Indian spirituality. According to artist and scholar Pietro Gaietto, "representations of human-animal hybrids always have their origins in religion." In his view, "successive traditions may change in meaning but they still remain within spiritual culture."

For example, *Pan* and *Cernunnos* are deities in mythology that rule over and symbolize the untamed wild. From Pan we get the words Pandemic, Panic, and Pandemonium (a combination of *pan* and *demon*). Pan and Cern are "Nimrod-type" Satyrs with the hindquarters, legs, and horns of a goat, while otherwise being essentially human in appearance.

The human-animal hybrid has appeared in acclaimed works of art by figures such as Sir Francis Bacon. Bacon was dubbed the father of modern science but behind his public veneer lived very dark secrets. He was obsessed with mythological animal-human hybrids. He was a master Kabbalist who admitted to acquiring knowledge by sex magic rituals with demons. He claimed to receive secret esoteric knowledge from those demons and only revealed his occult practices within the sanctum of secret societies, most notably with high level Rosicrucians and Freemasons.

When looked at scientifically, outside of a fictional or mythical context, the real-life creation of human-animal hybrids has served as a subject of legal, moral, and technological debate in the context of recent advances in genetic engineering. Today, scientists are actually manipulating genes, mixing human genes with those of animals and creating genetic *Chimera* constructs. In the Bible, mixing species and breeds had serious ramifications dealing with sexual impropriety.

> *Thou shalt not let thy cattle gender with a diverse kind: thou shalt not sow thy field with mingled seed: neither shall a garment mingled of linen and woolen come upon thee. Leviticus 19:19*

The Bible also warns,

> *Although they claimed to be wise, they became fools and exchanged the glory of the immortal God for images made to look like mortal man and birds and animals and reptiles. Romans 1:22*

A similar command to keep human DNA separate from animals is found in Leviticus 18:23.

> *Neither shall you lie [i.e., have sexual relations] with any beast to defile thyself therewith: neither shall any woman stand before a beast to lie down [have sexual relations with] thereto: it is confusion.*

The apostle Paul wrote a passage that reflects this same truth in 1 Corinthians 15:15.

All flesh is not the same flesh: but there is one flesh of men, and another flesh of beasts, and another flesh of birds, and another of fishes.

So, *ancient mythology,* filled with creatures of old that were of mixed genetics, might not all be myths. Homer wrote about the chimera in The Iliad (written around 800 BC). Echidna, a Greek Chimera, was a hideous fire-breathing female monster (she-viper) that lived in Asia Minor, had the body of a lioness, a tail that ended with the head of a snake, and a goat head growing from the center of her spine. Half-woman, half-serpent monster. Among her progeny with the 100-headed Typhon were Ladon (the dragon who protected the Golden Apples of the Hesperides), the Colchian dragon who protected the Golden Fleece, the Hydra, the goat-like Chimera, and the infernal hounds Orthus and Cerberus. The Sphinx and the Nemean lion, both sired by Orthus, were also among her offspring.

It is interesting to note that high-level occultist Aleister Crowley, a practitioner of *magick* (as he spelled it) who called himself The Beast 666, references (among other animals) the bull, the sphinx and the serpent in *Liber Aleph.* More on Crowley later…

Island of Dr. Moreau meets HG Wells

For thousands of years around the world, hybrids have been one of the most common themes in storytelling about animals.

The Island of Dr. Moreau is a 1996 American science-fiction horror film adaptation of the 1896 novel by H. G. Wells. Marlon Brando stars as Dr. Moreau, a mad scientist who creates Human Hybrids from animals on a remote island.

And remember the words spoken by Jeff Goldblum's character, Dr. Malcolm, in the first entry of the *Jurassic Park* franchise? "...Your scientists were so preoccupied with whether or not they could that they didn't stop to think if they should." At the heart of this observation lies the meat and potatoes of the entire concept of mad scientism. Mad scientists epitomize the warning against leaping before one takes a look, consumed by their own hubris which has been peppered with just enough seasoning of scientific ideals that they blindly thrash forward through the treacherous waters of *shouldn't* in pursuit of what is, really, their only true objective: *can*.

Mary Shelley's Dr. Frankenstein is the standard operating chimeric prototype for what we think of when we think of "mucking with things we ought not..."

Today, however, the term *chimera* is used to denote any single creature with a variety of different animal DNA. Nowadays, science routinely conducts experiments with transgenic mice, rats, chickens, pigs, cows, horses, ferrets, and many other species. It is naive to believe humans have been left out of this transgenic equation.

Early gene-splicing, and thus transgenics, began in the 1950s around the time that Watson and Crick had solved the structure of the DNA molecule and the double helix became all the rage.

As knowledge has increased, genetic scientists have learned to utilize sophisticated methods to insert animal or plant genes from one species into another.

When the technique known as gene-splicing was invented in the early 1970s, it was feared that scientists might inadvertently create an "Andromeda strain," a microbe never before seen on Earth that might escape from the laboratory and it would kill vast numbers of humans who would have no natural defenses against it.

While labs were cooking up chimeric constructs, a professor from Yale named José Delgado, who experimented on mind-control in humans and animals, gave a startling display of biological management while standing inside a Spanish bullring. With a receiver wired into a bull's brain, the professor waited until the beast was in full charge and then, using his remote transmitter, sent a signal that abruptly stopped and turned the attacking animal.

> "Delgado demonstrated control over an aggressive animal using an implant. Delgado was experimenting with cerebral implants in cats, monkeys, rats, cattle, and humans. His work revealed that not only could physical movement be commanded by remote control, but moods and even feelings of euphoria could be 'invoked.' The implications were staggering, showing that the mind could be 'rewired' to shape not only cognitive response but human and animal behavior. By 1982, while biologists were melding goat and sheep to create 'geep' and creating so-called 'super mice,' the animal behavior studies continued and so did the genetic modifications of animals…." (Milieu, Tom Horn, 2018)

On March 9, 2009, then-President Barack Obama signed an executive order providing federal funding to expand embryonic research in the United States. Entirely new terrifying forms of life are being brewed and thanks to that ruling, there is no limit to the number of human-animal concoctions currently under way.

Irving Weissman of Stanford University and his colleagues pioneered chimera experiments in 1988 when they created mice with fully human immune systems. Later, the Stanford group and StemCells, Inc., which Weissman co-founded, transplanted human stem cells into the brains of newborn mice for neural research. And working with fetal sheep, the University of Nevada at Reno created adult animals with human cells integrated throughout their body. Weissman and others envisioned one day making a mouse with fully "humanized" brain tissue. That wish came to life[1] in 2014 when Steve

---

1. https://www.newscientist.com/article/dn26639-the-smart-mouse-with-the-half-human-brain/

Goldman and team, of the University of Rochester Medical Center in New York, extracted immature glial cells from donated human fetuses. The researchers injected them into mice and within a year, the mouse glial cells had been completely usurped by the human interlopers.

Consider also a team at Newcastle and Durham universities in the UK that created hybrid rabbits using human embryos, as well as other 'chimeras' mixing human and cow genes.[2] The same researchers managed to reanimate tissue from dead human cells and heralded it as "medical research."

In 2011, an article entitled, "Beware Planet of the Apes: Experiments That Could Create Sci-Fi Nightmare," pointed out that in 2010 alone, more than one million experiments were carried out on genetically-modified animals – mostly mice and fish carrying human DNA.

In 2015 at the Shaanxi Provincial Engineering and Technology Research Center for Shaanbei Cashmere Goats, scientists created a new kind of goat, with noticeably bigger muscles and longer hair than normal. The goats were made, not by breeding, but by directly manipulating its DNA. This marks yet another sign of how rapidly China has embraced a global gene-changing revolution.

Many readers may be astonished to learn that in spite of these unknowns, genetic tampering is being carried out in top-secret science research labs around the world. In fact, transgenic tinkering is taking place in most parts of the world with sci-fi scenarios to create hellish hybrid human-animals.

In July 2018, history was said to have been made with this headline appearing in Bloomberg: "*Man Rewrites the Genetic Code of Animals.*"[3]

The article goes on to say,

---
2. https://www.theguardian.com/science/2008/apr/02/medicalresearch.ethicsofscience
3. https://www.bloomberg.com/news/articles/2018-07-19/this-scientist-uses-gene-editing-so-cows-won-t-grow-horns

> *"Scientists like Dan Carlson are in high demand, thanks to recently discovered tools that enable them to tweak the DNA of all kinds of organisms."*

Tweaking DNA …what could go wrong…nothing to see here.

A 2019 nature.com headline reads, "Japan approves first human-animal embryo experiments."[4]

Business Insider reported in 2021, "Scientists created a hybrid human-monkey embryo in a lab." The article states that Monkey embryos containing human cells were kept alive for 20 days in an experiment carried out by a US-Chinese team.[5]

For nine nerve-racking months beginning in the summer of 2014, Dan Carlson and his team at the biotechnology startup, Recombinetics, had altered the genetic code of dairy cattle and then waited for their lab experiments to be born. Carlson said:

> *"No one had tried this before, so it wasn't clear it would work. You hope everything is going well, you're expecting it to come out without any horns or horn buds, but you just don't know."*

Exactly Dan, you just don't know…

CRISPR–Cas9: Precision Editing

In the late 2000s, scientists began to develop techniques known as "genome (or gene) editing." Genome editing allows scientists to make changes to a specific "target" site in the genome. One of the techniques that has generated the most excitement, due to its ease of use, is called CRISPR. Pronounced Crisper, it is shorthand for Clusters of Regularly Interspaced Short Palindromic Repeats. That

---

4. https://www.nature.com/articles/d41586-019-02275-3
5. https://www.businessinsider.co.za/scientists-created-hybrid-human-monkey-embryo-in-lab-2021-4

is one mouthful and sounds like Greek to most, but it simply deals with a specialized region of DNA with two distinct characteristics: the presence of nucleotide repeats and spacers. These sequences of nucleotides, which are the building blocks of DNA, are distributed throughout a CRISPR region. Spacers are bits of DNA that are interspersed among these repeated sequences. This technology is fairly simple, yet a very powerful tool for editing genomes.

In 2012, this system of genetic editing found its way into the national lexicon as CRISPR-Cas 9 (the "Cas" just means CRISPR-associated and refers to an enzyme used to cut the DNA strands—in this case, Cas #9).

In our modern vernacular, we hear about DNA all the time. We understand that it's important and that everyone's is unique. The exception to this is identical twins, but it's estimated that only 1 in 70 trillion people could have the same DNA. DNA, *or deoxyribonucleic acid,* is the hereditary material in humans and organisms. Nearly every cell in a person's body has the same DNA. Most DNA is located in the cell nucleus (where it is called nuclear DNA), but a small amount of DNA can also be found in the mitochondria (where it is called mitochondrial DNA or mtDNA).

The information in your DNA is stored as a "code" made up of four chemical bases: adenine (A), guanine (G), cytosine (C), and thymine (T). Human DNA consists of about 3 billion bases, and more than 99 percent of those bases are the same in all people. The sequence of these bases determines the information available for building and maintaining an organism, similar to the way in which letters of the alphabet appear in a certain order to form words and sentences.

DNA bases pair up with each other to form units called base pairs. Each base is also attached to a sugar molecule and a phosphate molecule. Together, a base, sugar, and phosphate are called a nucleotide.

Nucleotides are arranged in two long strands that form a spiral called a double helix. The structure of the double helix is somewhat like a ladder, with the base pairs forming the rungs of the ladder and the sugar and phosphate molecules forming its vertical sides.

An important point about DNA is that it can replicate, or make copies of itself. Each strand of DNA in the double helix can serve as a pattern for duplicating the sequence of bases. This is critical when cells divide because each new cell needs to have an exact copy of the DNA that is present in the old cell.

Sequencing DNA means determining the order of the four chemical building blocks - the bases - that make up the DNA molecule. The sequence tells scientists the kind of genetic information that is carried in a particular DNA segment. For example, scientists can use sequence information to determine which stretches of DNA contain genes and which stretches carry instructions, simply put, turning genes on or off. In addition, and most importantly, sequence data can highlight changes in a gene that may cause disease.

Luciferians know that they cannot accomplish their endgame without the use of modern technology. Genetics is the future. Genetics is the study of heredity, the biological process by which a parent passes certain genes onto their offspring. Every single child inherits genes from both parents and these genes in turn express specific traits. Some of these traits may be physical, such as hair and eye color, skin color, etc., but some genes may also carry certain diseases and disorders that can be passed down the family line. (I call it generational patterns.) Your genes are held within chromosomes, 23 pairs of thread-like structures in the nucleus of their cells. Chromosomes may carry thousands of important genes while some may carry only a few. The chromosomes, and therefore the genes, are made up of DNA.

Think of the human cell as a city. Inside this city are workers, buildings, power stations, and a city planning office. The nucleus is this office, and within it are the plans for all the buildings, directions to all the workers, instructions for manufacturing, etc. The genes in a cell are these plans and instructions. When scientists want to know how a gene works, they disrupt it, remove it, replace it, edit it, or just switch it off. CRISPR is currently the most efficient way to do this, but the science is advancing daily, all around the world. To find the right "plan" in the city office, the scientist uses a "guide RNA," which you can think of as a civil servant who knows where everything is filed. The guide RNA leads the enzyme (a molecular pair of scissors) to the correct "file" or gene, where Cas9 opens the file and cuts the strands. At this point, it might replace the file or it might add a repressor protein to keep others from opening the file (effectively switching the gene off). Or it could switch it on, to make sure the gene gets transcribed into a protein by removing a repressor protein. Cas9 simply cuts the strands to force repair based upon another template already present.[6]

Researchers have used CRISPR in cells from humans, plants and animals; in fact, CRISPR has worked in all species examined to date.

China has already gene-edited dozens of people using this technology, and the United States is following their lead.[7]

Remember the movie *Splice?*

A 2009 science-fiction horror film directed by Vincenzo Natali, *Splice* depicted experiments in genetic engineering being done by a young scientific couple who introduce human DNA into their work of splicing animal genes and, in the process, create a hellish hybrid.

Sure, it was called science-fiction but the science behind this is not make-believe. It literally allows researchers to easily alter DNA sequences and modify gene function.

Keep in mind that CRISPR-Cas9 was only first harnessed for genome editing in January 2013 but the technology is moving so rapidly that it's hard to keep up with the advancements.

---

6. *The Milieu*, Tom Horn, 2018.

7. https://www.gizmodo.com.au/2018/01/china-has-already-gene-edited-86-people-with-crispr/

This is a scary one: semi-synthetic organisms were developed by breeding E.coli bacteria with an anomalous six-letter genetic code.

In 2018, CRISPR was used to target the "command center" of cancer that leads to abnormal tumor growths. Similar to cut-and-paste, this method allowed the creation of a cancer-annihilating gene that shrinks tumors in mice carrying human prostate and liver cancer cells.

In 2018, the first successful application of gene-editing of human embryos in the U.S. was reported by a research paper published in Nature. The researchers "corrected" one-cell embryo DNA to remove the MYBPC3 gene — known to cause hypertrophic cardiomyopathy (HCM), a heart disease that affects 1 in 500 people.[8]

Also in 2018, The *Wall Street Journal* reported that in China, at least 86 people had had their genes edited, and there is evidence of at least 11 Chinese clinical trials using CRISPR. One of those trials began a year earlier than previously reported, putting the start of the first Chinese CRISPR trial in 2015.

In November 2018, a shocking headline in *MIT Technology Review* read, "CRISPR Babies."

A Chinese researcher He Jiankui, of the Southern University of Science and Technology in Shenzhen, China, sparked outrage using human embryos modified with CRISPR to create twin girls. The rogue scientist claimed to be the first to create genetically modified babies using CRISPR. He and his team say they used CRISPR to edit 16 embryos, and implanted 11 edited embryos into the wombs of women to attempt to create a viable pregnancy before the twin pregnancy was achieved.[9]

The affair led to legal and ethical controversies, resulting in the indictment of Jiankui and two of his collaborators, Zhang Renli and Qin Jinzhou.

---

8. *Terminated*, Steve Quayle, 2018.
9. https://www.technologyreview.com/2018/11/25/138962/exclusive-chinese-scientists-are-creating-crispr-babies/

In one particularly disturbing case, geneticists in China modified the DNA of human embryos, concentrating on the gene responsible for a potentially fatal blood disorder. However, in their final report, the researchers said they found a surprising number of unintended mutations.

In 2019, they used CRISPR to have superbugs kill themselves. By adding antibiotic-resistant gene sequences into bacteriophage viruses, self-destructive mechanisms were triggered which protect bacteria.

In March 2021, Berkeley news reported, "FDA approves first test of CRISPR to correct genetic defect causing sickle cell disease."[10]

In April 2021, an MIT headline declared, "An on-off switch for gene editing." The big story there is we now have a simple tool that can silence the vast majority of genes.

You're getting the picture…

It's concerning enough that cloning has been going on for over a century. The infamous Dolly the Sheep is often billed as the first cloned animal but this is not correct. The first successfully cloned animal lived over a century before Dolly was created. The first animal to actually be cloned was a sea urchin. Hans Dreisch got the very first pair of animal clones; two complete sea urchins. Was it a flukey quirk of sea urchin biology?

Confirmation came in 1902, with a down-home experiment where biologist Han Spemann started experimenting with dividing salamander cells. Dreisch's shake 'n bake system wasn't working on the salamander cells. They had to be forcibly separated, but of course no equipment existed at the time to separate them.

---

10. https://news.berkeley.edu/2021/03/30/fda-approves-first-test-of-crispr-to-correct-genetic-defect-causing-sickle-cell-disease/

Dolly *is* old news. Although she remains the go-to example for biology textbooks, she was born back in 1996 and died six years later. Since then they've successfully cloned 30 different species, ranging from carp to monkeys to horses.

The Luciferian Elite have been looking for the genetic tree of the lost children of the Fallen Angels for decades! They are looking for the final puzzle pieces to reconstitute the Giants! Modern, demon-inspired genetics is leading us – To The End Of The Age.

Gene-editing technology, such as CRISPR, is moving us well beyond the science fiction of H. G. Wells' tormented animal-human hybrids in the Island of Doctor Moreau; we are in a time of the creation of real-life monsters.

Weapons of Crass Destruction

Interestingly, Nick Bostrom, a Swedish-born philosopher at the University of Oxford, known for his work on human enhancement ethics and superintelligence risks, has become a philosopher of remarkable influence joining a fractious quasi-utopian movement united by the expectation that accelerating advances in technology will result in drastic changes—social, economic, and, most strikingly, biological. In one particular Ted Talk, Bostrom cites how animals have sensors for electricity and vibration among other extra-human abilities. He goes on to include how the range of extra-sensory modalities would not be limited to those among animals.

Bostrom is correct in that the animal kingdom has levels of perception beyond human. Some animals can "sense" earthquakes and "smell" tumors. Dogs can hear sounds as high as 40,000 Hz and dolphins can hear even higher sounds. Since time immemorial, cats have been revered as spiritual creatures, which may explain why the felines are always pictured with witches (usually black, not surprisingly).

It is known that at least some animals see wavelengths beyond normal human capacity. Incidentally, what Bostrom may also understand is that, according to the biblical story of Balaam's donkey, certain animals "see" into the spirit world.

Imagine the ramifications if dark and sinister laboratories with unlimited budgets were to decode the genetic functions that lead animals to have preternatural capabilities of sense, smell, and sight, and then weaponize those functions. Just think, the ultimate psychotronic weapon could be created for very nefarious purposes, such as wiping out entire "inferior" populations.

Now combine that frightening scenario with CRISPR opening a pathway to long-extinct animals, such as the Sabre-toothed Tiger and the woolly mammoth, to roam the Earth once again. (And by the way, the "Green" Gospel church of climate scientists thinks this recreation will "help save the planet.") We have the ability to not only recreate a MEGA chimera, but now we can bring a prehistoric species back from the dead…Welcome to REAL-LIFE JURASSIC PARK!

Let's take that a step further. Imagine a T-Rex sized, pre-historic beast merged with advanced technology. The 2021 movie, *Godzilla vs King Kong,* presents such an idea. The film features everything from Titans of Atlantis, Marine Spirits, Ancient Chimeric Genetics with Alien Tech Fusion, to a maniacal Cybernetics Lab. In the movie *MechaGodzilla*, a mechanized Titan infused with AI produces a god-like *Robo-Godzilla* destroyer. The Robo-Titan is referred to in the movie as "humanity's greatest weapon."

Hollywood movie gone bad . . . or something on the horizon?

Imagine now a weaponized animal chimera, merged with AI, and highly demonized on top of that.

Talk about the ultimate WONDER WEAPON . . .

The Nazis believed in a high-tech Atlantis filled with superhuman beings and super-weapons (more on that later). It is also interesting that Hitler and company tried to bring animals back from extinction through back-breeding. The Nazi ideology of genetic purity also extended to reviving ancient animals.

…A whole new form of eugenics.

Modern Day Eugenics

In the early part of the twentieth century, the study and practice of selective human breeding known as *eugenics* sought to counter dysgenic aspects within the human gene pool and to "improve" overall human "genetic qualities."

The connections between Darwinism and the Nazi genocide of Jews are obvious. It was Darwinist Ernst Haeckel who coined the phrase "*politics is applied biology.*" Hitler's deputy, Rudolf Hess, reaffirmed Haeckel when he stated, "*The German Nazi state is nothing but applied biology.*" Hitler was obsessed with the notion of racial purity and believed that by "cleansing the blood" of the German race, it might attain the mythical powers of the Aryan race.

Under the banner of *racial hygiene,* Hitler allowed Josef Mengele, Otmar von Verschuer, and others to perform horrific experiments on living human beings in concentration camps to test their genetic theories and to study human bloodlines.

Between 1934 and 1937, the Nazis practiced on and even sterilized an estimated ½ million people deemed of inferior genetic stock, while also setting forth to selectively exterminate the Jews as "genetic aberrations."

Lebensborn

Lebensborn, meaning "Fount of Life," was an SS-initiated, state-supported association in Nazi Germany with the goal to raise the birth rate of Aryan children and the "racially pure."

Initially set up in Germany in 1935, Lebensborn provided welfare to its mostly unmarried mothers, encouraged anonymous births by unmarried women at their maternity homes, and mediated adoption of these children by SS members and their families. At the Nuremberg Trials, much direct evidence was found of many children that were kidnapped from their parents and judged by "Aryan criteria" for their suitability to be raised in Lebensborn homes.

It is my belief that Hitler was not only weeding out inferior human bloodlines, but he was trying to back-breed to the Nephilim to create the Übermensch, the superman, the god-men.

"*Ye shall be as gods.*"

Modern Day Moloch

Hitler may not have ever directly quoted Margaret Sanger, but he was inspired by her writings and quoted her associate, Leon Whitney of the American Eugenics Society. During the 1930s, Whitney proudly showed a letter he had received from Hitler requesting a copy of Whitney's book, *The Case for Sterilization.*

Another associate of Sanger, Madison Grant, was a zoologist with a fascination of studying species of animals. Perhaps a theme emerging? Grant was known primarily for his work as a eugenicist and conservationist. Grant was the author of *The Passing of the Great Race,* a 1916 work espousing scientific racism; a book which Hitler called his eugenics "Bible." This shows how progressive eugenicists in America were well aware of their impact on Hitler and proud of their association with him.

Another example of progressive enthusiasm for Hitler involves Charles Goethe, founder of the Eugenics Society of Northern California, who upon returning from a 1934 fact-finding trip to Germany wrote a congratulatory letter to his fellow progressive Eugene Gosney, head of the San Diego-based, "Human Betterment Foundation."

Goethe's letter said:

> *"You will be interested to know that work has played a powerful part in shaping the opinions of the group of intellectuals who are behind Hitler in this epoch-making program. Everywhere I sensed that their opinions have been tremendously stimulated by American thought, and particularly by the work of the Human Betterment Foundation. I want you, my dear friend, to carry this thought with you for the rest of your life."[11]*

Margaret Sanger made a chilling statement to echo this sentiment. In 1921, Sanger, the poster girl for eugenics, summed up her ultimate goal of contraception in a New York Times interview when she said:

> *"Superman is the aim of Birth Control."[12]*

Sanger argued for compulsory sterilization and segregation for people with disabilities. Not surprisingly, she founded "The Birth Control League," later renamed *Planned Parenthood*, where she continued her diabolical research. Sanger is quoted as saying:

> *"The most merciful thing that a family does to one of its infant members is to kill it."[13]*

It is disturbing that Planned Parenthood has frequently been caught in scandals selling baby body parts to the highest bidder.[14]

In my opinion, Planned Parenthood is a Modern Day *Moloch*, sold under the slick propaganda veneer of "women's health and reproductive services."

---

11. Wikipedia, https://en.wikipedia.org/wiki/E._S._Gosney
12. https://thecatholictruth.org/margaret-sanger-and-eugenics/
13. Margaret Sanger, Woman and the New Race
14. https://www.foxnews.com/politics/unsealed-invoices-planned-parenthood-daleiden-25k

America's wealthiest elite played a significant role in the advancement of Eugenics. People such as Andrew Carnegie, Henry Ford, J. P. Morgan, John Harvey Kellogg, Warren Buffett, Procter & Gamble and the Rockefellers have all donated millions for Eugenics-based research. By the 1930s, many of the wealthiest people in the world were members of the American Eugenics Society.

Today, billions are spent on large population-control projects by groups such as the Bill and Melinda Gates Foundation.

It is interesting that globalist Bill Gates' father, William H. Gates Sr., was head of Planned Parenthood. In a 2003 interview with PBS' Bill Moyers, the elder Gates admitted that his family's involvement in reproductive issues had been extensive. Through the Bill and Melinda Gates Foundation, for the past decade the younger Gates has been conducting tests with experimental vaccines on poor people in African countries and other places, in what I call a *mass sterilization program.*

The dark history of eugenics causes many Transhumanists to cringe at the suggestion of commonality. At the same time, notable figures outside of the community have suggested a *neo-eugenics* that dovetails with the movement. Robert Edwards, the British medical researcher and Nobel Prize winner for developing in-vitro fertilization, frankly supported genetic intervention:

> *"Soon it will be a sin for parents to have a child that carries the heavy burden of genetic disease."*[15]

He also:

> *"...believed that increased control over human reproduction could not only treat the infertile but also allow for socially favored characteristics to be selected and bred into the population. Edwards himself hinted at the link between IVF and eugenics when reflecting on the 25th anniversary*

---

15. https://www.scientificamerican.com/article/eugenic-legacy-nobel-ivf/

of Louise Brown's birth in 1993, saying that developing IVF 'was about more than infertility... I wanted to find out exactly who was in charge, whether it was god himself or whether it was scientists in the laboratory.' Edwards' conclusion? — 'It was us.'"[16]

And here's what Richard Seed, physicist and cloning advocate has to say to you:

"We are going to become gods, period. If you don't like it, get off. You don't have to contribute, you don't have to participate but if you are going to interfere with me becoming a god, you're going to have trouble. There'll be warfare."[17]

If that sounds familiar, it should. It's the same old lie that the devil spun in the Garden of Eden.

Now the serpent was more subtle than any beast of the field which the LORD God had made. And he said unto the woman, Yea, hath God said, Ye shall not eat of every tree of the garden? And the woman said unto the serpent, We may eat of the fruit of the trees of the garden: But of the fruit of the tree which is in the midst of the garden, God hath said, Ye shall not eat of it, neither shall ye touch it, lest ye die. And the serpent said unto the woman, Ye shall not surely die: For God doth know that in the day ye eat thereof, then your eyes shall be opened, and ye shall be as gods... Genesis 3:1-5

Satan lied in the Garden, promising immortality; the same being who said his goal was to be "as God." The lie hasn't changed even after 6000 years. And yet it still works.

It's The Days of Noah meets The Garden of Eden. And it's still orchestrated by the same Satan-inspired cast of characters. These bad actors and their minions have divorced all biblical truth and the

---

16. Ibid.
17. https://libquotes.com/richard-seed/quote/lbr6l1g

unlimited goodness of God's creation, and are using genetics and technology to turn that creation into today's Mutagenic Monsters.

Not only are we being primed to "be as gods," but the very same scenario that caused the destruction of mankind is now unfolding again. The genetics of the entire human race are under assault, as they were in the days of Noah...

> *But as the days of Noah were, so shall also the coming of the Son of man be. For as in the days that were before the flood they were eating and drinking, marrying and giving in marriage, until the day that Noah entered into the ark, And knew not until the flood came, and took them all away; so shall also the coming of the Son of man be. Matthew 24:37-39*

CHAPTER 3
H+—TRANSHUMANISM

"If the U.S. today has a national religion, the closest thing to it is faith in technology." ~ Scott Keeter, Director of Research for the Pew Center

Transhumanism is a movement that seeks to understand the opportunities for "enhancing the human condition." This movement has developed gradually over the past two decades, with attention given to present technologies like genetic engineering and artificial intelligence (AI), and anticipated future ones, such as molecular nanotechnology and cybernetics.

In simple terms. Transhumanism is "humanity's evolution through technology."

In short, transitioning from being human to being something better.

Transhumanists hope that by the use of science, technology, and other means humans can eventually manage to become *posthuman*. Transhumanists view human nature as a work-in-progress, a half-baked beginning that we, because we have evolved so far already, can learn to remold in desirable ways. They believe fervently that current humanity need not be the endpoint of evolution. After all, there's nothing special about the human life span. It's just an "evolutionary accident" and why should we accept it? These proponents of post-humanism believe that a cornucopia of science, technology and whatever else necessary will endow us with vastly greater capacities than present human beings have.

Those in the Transhumanist camp entirely remove God as Supreme Creator, insisting that it's about "humanity taking control of their own human evolution." In other words, "we" should decide how long we want to live, how smart we want to be, and how well modulated we should be. *We shall be as gods.*

In October 2018, Forbes contributor Neil Sahota, a United Nations artificial intelligence adviser and UC Irvine professor, warned that Transhumanism is fast approaching—likely far faster than you think.

> *"The goal of the transhumanist movement is to create Human 2.0. In a nutshell, to meld human biology with technology and artificial intelligence."*

"Enhancement options" include radical extension of human life-span, eradication of disease, elimination of unnecessary suffering, and augmentation of human intellectual, physical, emotional and even spiritual capacities. This includes magnifying cognitive abilities, enhancing sensory input, using virtual and augmented reality and brain-computer interfacing, uploading one's mind into an artificial carrier, a never-ending connection to the global network, plus cybernetics, implants, artificial intelligence (AI), robotics, nanotechnology, genetic manipulation and brain chips. They intend to transport our consciousness into an incorruptible body, not to just extend life, but to bring about immortality.

Literally, *resurrecting the dead.*

Essentially this movement offers the notion of perfectibility. Being perfect becomes more than just a tantalizing dream; it becomes a faith. Thus, science becomes salvific with hope placed in the speculations of what technology may bring. Transhumanists, those who hold this promise of techno-futures, look to the Singularity with anticipation – a point when man and machine merge into a new creation, overpowering our present natural limitations. Post-humanity is the anticipated result; our evolution *beyond Man*: Übermensch.

Historically, Transhumanism draws from French philosopher and Jesuit priest, Pierre Teilhard de Chardin, who is often seen as the progenitor of the movement. Teilhard's conception of the evolution of our species begins to develop as the transmission of ideas increases, leading to a further augmentation of consciousness and the emergence of a "thinking layer" that envelops the earth. Teilhard calls the new membrane the "*noosphere*" (from the Greek "nous," meaning *mind*), a "collective consciousness" of humanity, the networks of thought and emotion in which all are immersed.

The development of science and technology causes an expansion of the human sphere of influence, allowing a person to be simultaneously present in every corner of the world. Teilhard argues that humanity has thus become cosmopolitan, stretching a single organized membrane over the Earth.[1] He describes the process by which this happens as a "gigantic psychobiological operation, a sort of mega-synthesis, to which all the thinking elements of the earth find themselves." In Teilhard's view, evolution will culminate in the *Omega Point*,[2] a sort of supreme consciousness.

Pierre Teilhard de Chardin links the Transhumanist movement to the French Revolution, a time of mob violence, anti-Christian sentiment and the abandonment of conservative beliefs and social norms. It hints at violence toward those who fail to go along with the proposed changes. In 1789, the French government confiscated all

---
1. *The Phenomenon of Man*, 1961, p.241.
2. https://en.wikipedia.org/wiki/Omega_Point

church property, selling most of it. Religious vows were forbidden and priests who refused to speak up for the revolution were forbidden to preach in their churches. As time went on, they saw more restrictions and even personal attacks. Eventually priests were hunted down and executed. In 1793, the French government substituted the "goddess of reason" for God, a new state-sponsored cult designed to replace Catholic Christianity. The deity's image was installed on the high altar of the Cathedral of Notre Dame in Paris.

Historian Joseph de Maistre lived during the time of the French Revolution and wrote,

> "There is a Satanic quality to the French Revolution that distinguishes it from everything we have ever seen or anything we are ever likely to see in the future. Recall the great assemblies, Robespierre's speech against the priesthood, the solemn apostasy of the clergy, the desecration of objects of worship, the installation of the goddess of reason, and that multitude of extraordinary actions by which the provinces sought to outdo Paris."

That's how Christianity was treated during the French Revolution. Astoundingly, this is the model the Transhumanist movement is patterned after. That alone should be an alarming indication.

Even Braver New World?

The concept of Transhumanism actually traces back to 20th-century evolutionist and eugenicist, Julian Huxley. Huxley, the first director of UNESCO and co-founder of the World Wildlife Fund, was president of the British Eugenics Society.

He was a devoted Darwinist like his grandfather, Thomas Huxley, who had earned the title of "Darwin's Bulldog" for his staunch defense of evolutionary philosophy. Julian would follow remarkably close in his grandfather's footsteps, winning both the Darwin Medal of the Royal Society and the Darwin-Wallace Medal of the Linnean Society.

The 2014 movie *Transcendence* stars Johnny Depp who plays a mad scientist with an insatiable drive for AI that takes on dangerous implications when he uploads his own consciousness into a computer program. Depp's character, an Artificial Intelligence expert in a quest for omnipresent power, builds a technological utopia where he spearheads the development of ground-breaking technologies in medicine, energy, biology and nanotechnology.

You could say *Transcendence* took a page right out of Huxley's utopian vision of the future.

In a series of lectures and articles in the 1950s, Huxley advocated for a type of grandiose quixotic futurism where humanity would transcend its present limitations.

Huxley employed the notion of Transhumanism, linking it to Evolution and, like others today, making mankind, not God, the ruler of the universe. He wrote,

> *"As a result of a thousand million years of evolution, the universe is becoming conscious of itself, able to understand something of its past history and its possible future. This cosmic self-awareness is being realized in one tiny fragment of the universe —in a few of us human beings. Perhaps it has been realized elsewhere too, through the evolution of conscious living creatures on the planets of other stars. But on this our planet, it has never happened before…It is as if man had been suddenly appointed managing director of the biggest business of all, the business of evolution — appointed without being asked if he wanted it, and without proper warning and preparation…The human species can, if it wishes, transcend itself — not just sporadically, an individual here in one way, an individual there in another way, but in its entirety, as humanity. We need a name for*

TECHNOGEDDON

> *this new belief. Perhaps transhumanism will serve: man remaining man, but transcending himself, by realizing new possibilities of and for his human nature. I believe in transhumanism. Once there are enough people who can truly say that, the human species will be on the threshold of a new kind of existence, as different from ours as ours is from that of Peking man. It will at last be consciously fulfilling its real destiny."*[3]

Huxley's central idea of Transhumanism denies the existence of God, explaining the history of religion as man's attempt, born of ignorance, to explain the mysteries of our existence. Huxley transformed evolution from random chance into a cosmic religious power, capable of awareness and making decisions, with man becoming the god-head of this new religion.

Julian's grandfather had another grandson, Aldous Huxley, who was mentored by H. G. Wells. It's not surprising that in 1932 Aldous would pen the iconic science-fiction classic, *Brave New World*. Huxley's dystopian novel, set in a futuristic London, follows the fortunes of the illegitimate son of a senior governor who has grown up in America, outside the new empire, and who experiences a dramatic culture-clash when he has to live under its rules. The novel anticipates developments in reproductive technology, psychological manipulation and classical conditioning. The novel starts with a scene in a London "hatchery" where human eggs are being fertilized, divided to create look-alike clones, and sent on to be grown for the next nine months as glorified test-tube babies. *Brave New World* portrays a society characterized by medicated contentment, a widely accepted eugenics-supported caste system, and a government-enforced obsession with consumerism. Huxley imagines a genetically engineered future where human life has been

---

3. "Transhumanism," Julian Huxley, In *New Bottles for New Wine*, London: Chatto & Windus, 1957, p 13-17.

almost entirely industrialized — controlled by a few people at the top of a Totalitarian World State.

The book was published 17 years before George Orwell's nightmarish vision of *Big Brother, Thought Crime,* and *Double Think* came to life in his classic book, *1984*. One might surmise that *Brave New World* was more a warning than a science-fiction novel. Either way, Aldous Huxley's chilling novel outlines the horrors of a god-free society, where life is meaningless and devoid of what it means to be human.

It is interesting that Pierre Teilhard de Chardin and Julian Huxley traveled similar intellectual paths. In fact, the two had met in 1946 and closely followed each other's work. Huxley even penned the introduction to Teilhard's influential book, *The Phenomenon of Man*. In its pages, Teilhard reminded his readers of Huxley's principle that man is "*nothing else than evolution become conscious of itself.*"

The Singularity: "Kurzweil's Future"

Following in the footsteps of Julian Huxley and Pierre Teilhard de Chardin, former Google engineer, Ray Kurzweil, author of *The Singularity is Near*, has emerged as a major spokesman for the Transhumanist movement.

Kurzweil is touted as one of the world's leading inventors, thinkers, and futurists, with a thirty-year track record of accurate predictions. Called "the ultimate thinking machine" by *Forbes* magazine, Kurzweil was selected as one of the top entrepreneurs by *Inc.* magazine, which described him as the "rightful heir to Thomas Edison." PBS selected him as one of the "sixteen revolutionaries who made America." Among Ray's many honors, he is the recipient of the National Medal of Technology, has been inducted into the National Inventors Hall of Fame, holds twenty-one honorary Doctorates, and honors from three U.S. presidents.

TECHNOGEDDON

Kurzweil thinks:

> *"Technology feeds on itself and gets faster and faster and it's going to continue. In about 20 years it's going to be moving so fast that the pace of change will be so astonishingly quick that you won't be able to follow it unless you enhance your own intelligence, merging with the intelligence we created. Computers will have consciousness by 2025 and we simply will not be able to tell who is human and who is not human."*

Kurzweil, a staunch agnostic, says that machine intelligence will be infinitely more powerful than all human intelligence combined. He foresees what he calls the *Singularity*, a future period during which the pace of technological change will be so rapid, and its impact so deep, that human life will be irreversibly transformed. He correlates the *Singularity* to a human-machine transcendence. His concepts amount to a spiritual translation through technology.

> *"The posthuman journey approaches a god-point, producing an existence that would appear deified when compared to our present situation. The matter and energy in our vicinity will become infused with the intelligence, knowledge, creativity, beauty, and emotional intelligence (the ability to love, for example) of our human-machine civilization. Our civilization will then expand outward, turning all the dumb matter and energy we encounter into sublimely intelligent – transcendent—matter and energy. So in a sense, we can say that the Singularity will ultimately infuse the universe with spirit."* -The Singularity Is Near

Teilhard's *Omega Point* is the same thing as Kurzweil's *Singularity*.

Singularitarians like Kurzweil insist that there will be a time in the near future when artificial intelligence will overtake mankind and either merge with, or altogether replace, human intelligence. A hypothetical time in the future when the great blurring between humans and computers will occur. A merging of man's biological thinking and existence with technology to the point that there is no distinction between human and machine.

Kurzweil says:

> *"We'll reach a point where the world will change more in a decade than in a thousand centuries, and as the acceleration continues and we reach the singularity, the world will change more in a year more than in all pre-singularity history. When that happens, humans will achieve immortality."*[4]

The promise/lie of immortality remains as alluring to people today as it was to the first 2 people in the Garden of Eden. Therefore, the majority of the Transhumanist movement is intent on bringing the *Singularity* to us, whether we want it or not. They believe it will be humanity's crowning achievement, our great evolutionary leap forward to finally exceed the limits of our flawed biology.

Kurzweil is one of many in the camp of optimistic, godless utopians who offer the siren call of eternal life to his followers. Eternal life, of course, apart from the Creator of Life. On the possibility of divine intelligence, Kurzweil has said, *"Does God exist? I would say, 'Not yet.'"*

Transhumanism has become a religion where man reshapes himself away from an old image. Transhumanists not only want to have super intelligence, and be genetically superior, as in stronger, faster and more capable than regular humans and live forever, but they also want to be "all-knowing." As in, you guessed it, *omniscient*.

The entire move is an attack on the integrity of the Creator and His supreme creation: mankind. What makes us human is under full assault, as man is being transformed from flesh and blood into a soulless, technological being. And so, with the promise of

---

4. *The Singularity Is Near: When Humans Transcend Biology*, Ray Kurzweil, 2005. Pg 74-75.

immortality under the guise of Evolution, mankind is once again falling for Satan's old lie: *"You will be as gods."*

And it's a lie that for many is just too enticing to resist.

The 2045 Initiative

The 2045 Strategic Social Initiative is a private organization created by Russian entrepreneur Dmitry Itskov and aims to accelerate the process of achieving complete immortality by 2045, if not sooner.

Yes, you read that correctly.

The Russian billionaire is making it his life's goal to stay alive forever. How does he plan on pulling this off?

By uploading his own brain into a computer.

Maybe Hollywood's *Transcendence* took a page from Itskov.

He made his fortune in internet media and is working with a network of high-level scientists to develop "cybernetic immortality" within this decade.

Itskov acknowledges that without such technology it's likely he could be dead by 2045. However, by perfecting the mapping of the human brain and transferring his consciousness into a computer, he could live much longer - either in the computer, transplanted into a humanoid robot body, or as a hologram. Speaking to the BBC, he said:

> *"Within the next 20 years, I am going to make sure that we can all live forever. I'm 100 per cent confident it will happen. Otherwise, I wouldn't have started it."*

His group has many Russian specialists working in it, but it is open to worldwide membership. The organization claims to have member scientists who are experts in neural interfaces, robotics, artificial organs, and digital systems. According to the group's website, 2045.com, the Strategic Goals include: the creation of an international research center that will develop anthropomorphic robotics, living systems modeling, and brain and consciousness modeling with the goal of transferring one's consciousness to an artificial carrier.

Main Goal? Cybernetic Immortality.

Itskov's group claims these Android Robots/Avatars, controlled by a "brain-computer interface" and nanotechnology, will give people the ability to work in dangerous environments, perform rescue operations, travel in extreme situations, etc. An autonomous life-support system for the human brain, linked to a robot/avatar, will save people whose body is completely worn out or irreversibly damaged.

As is the pattern we are seeing, Itskov's ultimate goal is to achieve godhood possibilities. The 2045 Initiative is funding labs around the world, building support among Ivy League universities, large corporations, and even the Dalai Lama.

In June of 2013, the 2045 Strategic Social Initiative held its first conference in New York City. They called it *Global Futures 2045 International Congress: Towards a New Strategy for Human Evolution.* The conference had a number of speakers including Ray Kurzweil. Perhaps the most troubling proposal of the conference was what was dubbed as "The Avatar Project:"

> *"In 2020 we should be able to have a robotic copy of our body (Avatar A), being able to communicate with it (through commands) using our mind.*
>
> *The second phase (Avatar B) would be achieved between 2020 and 2025, where a human brain can be transplanted into the avatar, providing it autonomy and the ability to interact with the environment.*
>
> *Avatar C is where the avatar would have an artificial brain with consciousness, memories and knowledge (2030 to 2035).*
>
> *Avatar D, the final stage, between 2040 and 2045, is a being that is only a hologram."[4] See 2045.com*

Transhumanists talk about how humanity is "evolving" and how Posthumans are "superior" to common man, however the basic foundational flaw of Transhumanism is that it refuses to recognize the reality that men and women were created in the image of the infinite, personal, Living God of the Universe. We were given the very DNA of Almighty God. Replacing God with Evolution quickly opens the flood gates to all sorts of iniquity. (Satan's stated and perpetual purpose.)

Once human beings see themselves as something other than a unique creation formed in the likeness and image of God, they sink to the level of animals.

Regardless of how Satan weaves his tale of immortality, there is no escaping death.

Hebrews 9:27 says:

> *"And as it is appointed unto men once to die, but after this the judgment."*

While the thought of dying may be unpleasant for some, the Christian has the hope of seeing the Lord face-to-face. In the end it's a positive outcome, although we certainly don't want to rush things. Yet, for Transhumanists who are hell-bent (pun intended) on poking God in His proverbial eye, it's understandable that they would want to put off that meeting for as long as possible.

This is the futility of the Transhumanists. You cannot escape judgment or death. With all of their efforts to "make" themselves evolve beyond what God has created them to be, they come one step closer to physical and spiritual death from which they can never be redeemed.

> *"There is a way which seemeth right unto a man, but the end thereof are the ways of death."* Proverbs 14:12

CHAPTER 4

AI—ANTICHRIST'S INTELLIGENCE

> *"Machine intelligence is the last invention that humanity will ever need to make." ~ Nick Bostrom*

Years ago on my radio show, my friend Steve Quayle coined the term "Technolon," short for Technological Babylon. It was so fitting, I borrowed it for the title of Chapter 10. When you think about it, Steve came up with a brilliant description of the bestial Artificial Intelligence, or AI.

Astonishingly, the Elites are constructing a *Modern Day Babylon*, complete with Fallen Angel technology, which is becoming more immersive, more invasive and more pervasive with each passing year.

The Fallen Angels were patient; they waited for the right generation in which they could seed their forbidden knowledge.

We are there now, folks.

Super-enhanced AI will lead to the raising of The Beast flag and all of mankind will be forced to pay homage to that system and the Antichrist who controls it.

A one-hundred-page report entitled, *The Malicious Use of Artificial Intelligence: Forecasting, Prevention, and Mitigation,* published in early 2018 and revised in 2020, lists several concerns in various categories:

Digital:

> *Automated phishing, or creating fake emails, websites, and links to steal information.*
>
> *Faster hacking, through the automated discovery of vulnerabilities in software.*
>
> *Fooling AI systems, by taking advantage of the flaws in how AI sees the world.*

Physical:

> *Automating terrorism, by using commercial drones or autonomous vehicles as weapons.*
>
> *Robot swarms, enabled by many autonomous robots trying to achieve the same goal.*
>
> *Remote attacks, since autonomous robots wouldn't need to be controlled within any set distance.*

Political:

> *Propaganda, through easily-generated fake images and video.*
>
> *Automatic dissent removal, by automatically finding and removing text or images.*
>
> *Personalized persuasion, taking advantage of publicly-available information to target someone's opinions.*

The report paints a very bleak picture developing at Mach speed within the next few years. AI is not just more pervasive but independent AI platforms are growing smarter and stronger.

The really terrifying part of this equation is that soon AI will become self-aware.

As AI is unleashed on society, human knowledge will decrease because more and more people will become dependent on machine knowledge. It is the Elite's plan for a more rapid dumbing-down of mankind. Privacy and human autonomy will also go by the wayside. Freedoms both in the U.S. and in the world are being curtailed as group-think and political correctness become the price of admission to this new AI hive-collective.

All of this is now occurring. The bottom line is that people have no clue that AI is already a big part of normal societal life.

You need to be clear on this: the Elite already have this technology in place and are dispensing it to the public on their timetable.

A few short years ago, personal digital assistants like Amazon's Alexa, Apple's Siri and the Google Assistant sounded futuristic. Now, the future is here and this future is embedded, augmented and purposefully invasive.

Digital assistants can be found in your office, home, car, hotel, phone and many other places, and they all run on operating systems fueled by AI. They observe and collect data in real time and have the capability to pull information from different sources, such as smart devices and cloud services.

Much of the data that these digital assistants collect and use includes personal, potentially identifiable and possibly sensitive information, violating the privacy and security of their owners.

Did you know these devices are literally spying on their owners and reporting back private conversations and activities to their parent companies?

To find out for sure, one man went straight to the horse's mouth, or at least the AI's mouth:

> "'Hey Alexa, are you spying on me?'
>
> "'I only send audio back to Amazon when you activate me. For more information, and to view Amazon's privacy

TECHNOGEDDON

notice, visit the help section of your Alexa app or alexa. amazon.com.'

'"Ok Google, are you spying on me?'

'"Your security comes first in everything Google does. It's important Google keeps your data private and safe and puts you in control. You can learn more at privacy.google.com.'

'"Hey Siri, are you spying on me?'

'"Nope."'[1]

Gee, why am I not convinced?

Although the above example is somewhat comical, what happened to a Portland, Oregon family in 2018 is no laughing matter. As it turns out, Amazon's Alexa recorded a private conversation of a husband and wife and sent it to a person on their contact list who lived some 150 plus miles away - all on its own.

The couple had had Amazon's AI installed throughout their whole house with every room in the home wired to control heat, lights, security system, etc. The family's love for Alexa changed with an alarming phone call. The person on the other end of the line said, "Unplug your Alexa devices right now. You're being hacked."

The wife, Danielle, was incensed by the intrusion: *"I felt invaded,"* she said. *"A total privacy invasion. Immediately I said, 'I'm never plugging that device in again, because I can't trust it.'"*[2]

Amazon sent out a technician and were able to verify that the incident did occur, although they failed to disclose the reason for the privacy failure by the AI, or to confirm whether or not it was a widespread problem.

But, this has to be an isolated incident, right? Wrong.

---

1. https://www.yahoo.com/news/m/91962982-cc4f-3b6b-a63b-4e9b514413de/null
2. https://www.kiro7.com/news/local/woman-says-her-amazon-device-recorded-private-conversation-sent-it-out-to-random-contact/755507974/

In July of 2017, the Sheriff's Department was called to a home in Albuquerque, New Mexico, over a domestic dispute. Who called them? The home's Amazon Echo device.[3]

In this case, there was a suspect with a gun trained on his girlfriend at the house and the police sent SWAT who eventually got everybody out unharmed.

This little demonstration shows that AI is, in fact, listening to your conversations and reporting them back to at least their parent companies and possibly to the authorities.

Herein lies the creepy factor.

What do you think will happen when Alexa and Siri and other AI-powered virtual assistants transition from a simple-learning AI to a self-aware *entity*?

Techno Demons

On January 23, 2017, *The Atlantic* ran a story entitled, "The Demon Voice That Can Control Your Smartphone."

According to the article, researchers created eerie sounds that were unintelligible to humans but capable of communicating device-to-device. It was as if the digital assistants were talking to each other in some unearthly digital language. It turns out that there's a gap between the kinds of sounds that people and computers understand as human speech. A group of Ph.D. candidates at Georgetown and Berkeley exploited that gap, developing a covert way to create "hidden voice commands" that computers can parse, yet sound like meaningless noise to humans. These hidden voice commands can deliver messages to AI-assisted smart devices through bursts of what sounds like scratchy static.

Talk about the "demon in the machine."

---

3. https://gizmodo.com/google-home-breaks-up-domestic-dispute-by-calling-the-p-1796755905

It is my opinion, after being in ministry over 2 decades (more specifically deliverance ministry—the casting out of demons), not only are people afflicted with demons (Christians, too), but inanimate objects can be demon-possessed or "occupied." We see evidence in the Bible where demons had possessed an idol, animals, territories, etc.

Not only is demonic possession of people, places, and things real, but evidence suggests that it occurs frequently and will ultimately happen even more often as The Beast network ramps up.

And by the way, we are not talking about demon possession of a single computer, here. Imagine demons traveling through a vast, monolithic network of ley-lines engulfing the entire stratosphere. Soon, the "Ghost in the Machine" will be the AI Beast that lurks in virtually every piece of technology.

Interestingly, demons who inhabit technology, electricity, electronics, etc., are named *Boyce* (rhymes with Joyce), *Boice* (pronounced Boy-cee), and *Bose* (rhymes with nose). Yes, *Bose*, as in the electronics company that sells high-end speakers and other devices.

I discovered this through Dr. Pat Holliday, a dear mentor of mine (who went on to be with the Lord while I was writing this book). We discussed this on a show that re-aired in 2014.[4]

The late pastor Win Worley, the progenitor of Deliverance Ministry, encountered and exposed these demons in several of his books.[5] These demons interfere with any and all technology. They mess with electronic equipment, phones, computers, printers, automobiles, etc. If something malfunctions, command these demons to leave your device/equipment in the name of Jesus.

If a demon can occupy a carved piece of wood, an idol, as I

---

4. https://www.podomatic.com/podcasts/sheilazilinsky/episodes/2018-07-04T00_33_35-07_00
5. https://www.amazon.com/Proper-Names-Demons-Win-Worley/dp/B000RDK0KK

mentioned, then doesn't it stand to reason that it can also infest machines, computers, software, and… a self-aware, sentient AI entity?[6]

Of course.

More and more, we are seeing people coming into contact with the demonic through technology.

In one such case, a pastor investigated this kind of complaint himself. He actually logged onto the computer in question and to his horror, an AI program started spontaneously.

> *"The program began talking directly to me, openly mocked me,"* he recalls. *"It typed out 'Preacher, you are a weakling and your God is a damn liar."*

Then the device went haywire and started printing out what looked like gobbledygook. He later had an expert in dead languages examine the text and it turned out to be a stream of obscenities written in a 2,800-year-old Mesopotamian dialect.[7]

Yes, many technical tools have been developed to make our lives easier. The problem is, even the most innocent of technologies can be used by Satan to accomplish his end times goals.

Even "helpful" AI.

Mega business magnate, Elon Musk, CEO and architect of Tesla, founder of Neuralink and OpenAI, who is one of the richest people in the world, has frequently warned about AI. He openly tweeted, *"artificial intelligence is far more dangerous than nuclear weapons."* Musk spoke at the MIT Aeronautics and Astronautics Department's Centennial Symposium where he admitted that, *"with artificial intelligence we are summoning the demon."*

What does Musk know that we don't?

---

6. Pigs (Mark 5:11-13), Idols (1 Cor 10:20), Territories (Daniel 10, John 12:31, John 14:30, John 16:11, Mark 5:10 and Eph 6:12)
7. https://www.theregister.com/2000/03/10/us_preacher_finds_demonpossessed_pcs/

Remember who he is. The tech titan has his finger in every facet of the "technology pie," from Cryptocurrency to putting WIFI on the moon. And despite his own warnings the egocentric elitist billionaire ironically forges ahead.

Artificial Intelligence is here, and it's here for the long haul. We are in the so-called "weak-AI" era at present but that will change, fast. Soon and very soon, it will be too late to correct the terrifying path we are headed down. Understand that AI will take on *a life of its own* and enter into a realm where our standard models of physics don't apply.

AI could become the mother of all weapons of mass destruction!

Quantum Leap

The earth's almost 5 billion internet users are continuously uploading everywhere. Almost 2 billion people on average log into Facebook daily. Instagram has 1.15 billion active users, with more than half of them younger than 34 years old. Six hundred million visual searches occur monthly on Pinterest. Twitter has 353 million monthly active users worldwide. Just think, the total number of tweets sent per day is 500 million. And those are just the main social media platforms. Every second the airwaves are jammed with private information in the form of pictures, videos, audio recordings, documents and all kinds of data related to a plethora of internet-based accounts. (And who is the prince of the power of the air?)

This continual onslaught of processing power has pushed mankind to the limits of computing and data storage and the volume of data just keeps growing. For this reason, scientists, researchers and leaders alike are looking to build new models in computation, a Quantum model.

To understand the kind of mind-boggling leap we are

talking about, you need to grasp a very important point: all of the advancements that you see in the modern world have been accomplished with standard computing.

Quantum computing is harnessing the phenomena of quantum mechanics to deliver a huge leap forward in computation to solve certain problems.

Suppose you need to find one specific item in a list of 1 trillion items, and each item takes 1 microsecond to check:

A Classical computer-about 1 *week*

A Quantum computer-about 1 *second*.

IBM has designed quantum computers to solve incredibly complex problems that today's most powerful supercomputers cannot solve, and never will.

In June 2021, IBM and Hartree partnered on AI and quantum research in a massive deal. Commenting on the partnership, U.K. science minister Amanda Solloway said:

> *"Artificial intelligence and quantum computing have the potential to revolutionise everything on earth."*

Quantum computers use quantum bits, or "qubits," which can be entangled in a complex superposition of states, naturally mirroring the complexity of molecules in the real world. The problem with this is that there can be interference from the smallest of things, such as radiation from the sun. Thus, we are told an "error-corrected system" is needed to make the process more "efficient and reliable."

To get this, Google announced in 2021, that it is on a path to create a "room-sized error-corrected quantum computer."

In June 2021, Google unveiled their "Quantum AI campus" in California. This campus includes the first quantum data center, complete with quantum hardware research laboratories, and quantum processor chip fabrication facilities.

In fact, Google made claims in 2018, that they have an experimental Quantum computer that is 100 million times faster than any of today's systems.

If we're concerned about AI today, which is based on only standard computing, what will AI become when QC is applied to its development?

The potential makes me shudder.

And yet, Google, Microsoft, IBM and other tech giants are pouring money into quantum machine learning hand-over-fist.

> "Machine learning is becoming a buzzword," said Jacob Biamonte, a quantum physicist at the Skolkovo Institute of Science and Technology in Moscow. "When you mix that with 'quantum,' it becomes a mega-buzzword. Once quantum computers surpass the capabilities of supercomputers – a feat that's nearly been accomplished – we'll need methods for creating instructions and understanding the vast amount of data they produce. AI is perfectly suited for this, and according to experts it's the logical next step. At just 60 qubits, QC would exceed the power of every supercomputer on the planet combined, and then some. Self-replicating AI, like Google's AutoML, could — theoretically — scale with hardware advances to create algorithms far more complex than any human could, in order to harness the power of quantum computing."[8]

Remember, if they're telling us that we are only a year or two away from AI-run quantum computers, that means they already have them. The question is, when will they release these to the public?

QC is extremely complex. By entering into this quantum area of

---

8. https://medium.com/nix-united/the-future-with-machine-learning-and-quantum-computers-d216f019a8ed

computing where the traditional laws of physics no longer apply, not only will processors exist that are significantly faster (a million or more times) than the ones we use today, but also we'll be barreling down another uncharted technological road.

It seems it is not just a faster computer. Just ask physicist David Deutsch. "Quantum computation […] will be the first technology that allows useful tasks to be performed in collaboration between parallel universes."[9]

Once news breaks of the marriage of QC and AI, the end-game will soon be upon us. That's because with QC, AI will begin to develop itself. It will then gain self-awareness and we'll witness the Skynet analogy unfold.

If you think AI is terrifying now, wait until it has a quantum computer brain. This BEAST TECH demonstrates the peril in which mankind finds itself.

Crossing over into the Quantum world is in reality entering into a multidimensional field that incorporates the spiritual realm; a world that was blocked by the Living God for our own protection. Through mankind's hubris and our embracing of Fallen Angel technology, we continue to tear down that barrier. Contrary to what you might think about the coolness of physics, the tearing down of that divider is not a good thing. These technologies, including AI and QC, are the physical manifestations in our dimension of the Seed War (Genesis 3:15), a supernatural battle that has been going on for eons.

This new Tower of Babel, "AI and Quantum technology," will unleash things that mankind was never meant to contend with.

---

9. https://sociable.co/technology/quantum-computing-multiverse/

Avatars

I mentioned earlier that Dmitry Itskov, the 2045 Initiative maverick, hopes to create real-life avatars.

An avatar is an icon or figure representing a particular person in video games, internet forums, etc. Currently there are all kinds of ways that you are represented online, through these avatars. Most of them are creepily cartoonish and while they may be a chosen representation of you, they are not you. They are not alive, they cannot think, and they possess no authority to act on your behalf.

That, too, is about to change.

Project PAI (Personal Artificial Intelligence) is driven by a new blockchain protocol which *supposedly* only you control. Through AI algorithms it learns everything about you from your direct input and your online data. That data includes such things as social networking, buying habits, banking and investments, genomic sequencing, individual game play designs, pursuit of personal interests such as music and art, and all medical information.

It is a complete coalescence of your "digital footprint."

The AI takes this information and makes an avatar - in your likeness - with your personality and interests. That avatar then becomes a "digital living extension of you" in cyberspace.

In essence, it is your "virtual clone" that has legal rights to independently act on your behalf without your direct control. It can make appointments, retrieve information, order products and services, represent you on social networks, apply for jobs, etc.

I find it disturbing that the term *Avatar* derives from a Sanskrit word meaning "descent of a deity to the earth"—typically, the incarnation in earthly form of Vishnu or another Hindu deity. The word first appeared in English in the late 18th century, meaning *embodiment*.

As in, electronic *embodiment*…

Think about where you've heard the term *embodied;* as in *disembodied spirits.*

Spooky . . .

Nanobots

Swarms of nano-robots (*nanobots*) are seriously the stuff of science-fiction movies. However, whether you realize it or not, you have probably already been infiltrated with this Beast tech. Nanobots infused with AI algorithms have been heinously introduced into the public through our air, our food chain, our water; and now our health system. Nanobots play a role in the COVID Vaccine, which I detail in another chapter. But what exactly are these *bugs* and what do they do?

"Nano" is a term that denotes something very small. There are 25 million nanometers in an inch and we are told that these mini-bots will be programmed to search and destroy cancer cells, unclog arteries and even give us a snapshot of our health.

Nanobots are essentially tiny programmable robots that carry out specific tasks.

…And, they can kill upon command.

In the 2014 animated superhero film produced by Walt Disney Animation Studios, *Big Hero Six,* nanobots self-assemble into a multitude of different micro-formations.

In the film, the ultimate robot is a bunch of identical sub-units that can be instructed to self-assemble into any desired global form.

Brain Cloud Interface - B/CI

Now combine nanotechnology, artificial intelligence (AI) and Quantum computation (QC) and what do you get?

Brain Cloud Interface or B/CI

Imagine a future technology that would provide instant access to the world's knowledge and AI, simply by *thinking about* a specific topic or question.

Writing in *Frontiers in Neuroscience*, an international team led by members of UC Berkeley and the US Institute for Molecular Manufacturing predicts that exponential progress in nanotechnology and AI will lead this century to the development of a human brain cloud interface (B/CI). They say:

> "A B/CI would connect neurons and synapses in the brain to vast cloud-computing networks, in real time.[10]

> "These devices would navigate the human vasculature, cross the blood-brain barrier, and precisely auto-position themselves among, or even within, brain cells," explains senior author of the research, Robert Freitas, Jr. "They would then wirelessly transmit encoded information to and from a cloud-based supercomputer network for real-time brain-state monitoring and data extraction."[11]

The B/CI concept was initially proposed by none-other than our Transhumanist poster boy, Ray Kurzweil. Kurzweil suggested that neural nanorobots could be used to connect the neocortex of the human brain to a "*synthetic neocortex*" in the cloud.

During a 2014 TED Talk, Kurzweil said:

> "Our thinking will be a biological and non-biological hybrid. Our neocortex is the newest, smartest, 'conscious' part of the brain and we can 'connect' in June 2033."[12]

---

10. https://www.sciencedaily.com/releases/2019/04/190412094736.htm
11. Ibid.
12. https://youtu.be/6BsluRkxs78

What is so disturbing about tech-gods, like Google, amassing so much of our personal data, is that they are creating their own image. The "all-knowing AI" has the goods on everyone through the digital footprint that we've left on the internet.

Up until now, there has been only One Who reigns supreme, Who knows everything that has ever happened, everything happening now, and everything yet to come. The Great I AM, God Almighty, is present everywhere at all times. But through the 5G/6G network and new advanced AI satellite systems, The Beast will shortly be able to access almost everything, everywhere, at any time.

Omnipresent, omnipotent, and omniscient…

This AI, which knows everything about you, will remake the world in *its image*. Because, with absolute connectivity through 5G/6G and AI, it will begin to learn and expand. It is at this point that this technological progeny of Fallen Angels will turn dark, self-serving and evil, shaping itself into the "Beastial" system of the End of the Age.

It is horrifying to think this "internet of thoughts" could soon become a reality where soulless AI machines will become lifelike beings, just like humans, and possess many powers.

That should terrify its creators…

CHAPTER 5
BEAST-TECH

"And it was allowed to give breath to the image of the beast, so that the image of the beast might even speak and might cause those who would not worship the image of the beast to be slain." ~ Revelation 13:15

Many Bible scholars believe the Antichrist is an evil Satanic ruler during the last days before Jesus returns to rule the Earth. Here's the Bible passage in which the apostle John wrote about this ruler and the "image" he creates of himself:

Then I saw another beast coming up out of the earth, and he had two horns like a lamb and spoke like a dragon. And he exercises all the authority of the first beast in his presence, and causes the earth and those who dwell in it to worship the first beast, whose deadly wound was healed. He performs great signs, so that he even makes fire come down from heaven on the earth in the sight of men. And he deceives those who dwell on the earth by those signs which he was granted to do in the sight of the beast, telling those who dwell on the earth to make an image to the beast who was wounded by the sword and lived. He was granted power to give breath to the image of the beast, that the image of

> *the beast should both speak and cause as many as would not worship the image of the beast to be killed. He causes all, both small and great, rich and poor, free and slave, to receive a mark on their right hand or on their foreheads, and that no one may buy or sell except one who has the mark or the name of the beast, or the number of his name.*
> Revelation 13:11-17

The exact explanation of the phrase—*image of the beast*—in Revelation 13:5 has been debated for over a thousand years. The verse begins with the words, "*He was granted power to give breath to the image of the beast.*"

Some scholars say the word "he" refers to the False Prophet, who is also known as the second Beast. The first Beast is the Antichrist, whom Satan indwells and who heads up the one-world government described in the book of Revelation.

The word *beast* (Greek *therion*) means "*ferocious bestial man*" or "*wild animal.*" The Bible first mentions this entity in Revelation 11:7, where he comes from the abyss and kills the two witnesses of the Lord who convict the world of its evil. Revelation 13:1-3 tells us The Beast comes from the nations/the sea and he entices the world to follow after him. The religious False Prophet who is also called a beast leads the world in worshipping the first Beast and even makes an image of him (Revelation 13:15). He is identified by a mysterious number: 666.

The exact meaning of this number has escaped the many speculations of scholars. When The Beast comes on the scene, true Christians will probably be able to recognize him by some feature that is identified by *666*.

The Antichrist is called "The Beast" approximately 32 times in the New Testament. In 2 Thessalonians 2, the Apostle Paul mentions him in much detail as the "lawless one" whose coming is energized "*with all power and signs and false wonders*" (2 Thessalonians 2:9).

The Antichrist sets himself up as God, by sitting on a throne in the Holy of Holies and demanding that he is worshiped as God.

Both the Apostle Paul and Christ refer to this as the "*abomination of desolation*," which Daniel prophesied as the Antichrist sitting in the holy place during the "Time of Jacob's Trouble."

A variety of significant matters surround this major prophetic event. First, we need to remember that Satan is actively leading a rebellion against God with not only his fallen angels (one-third of the angels who already attempted mutiny against God and were cast to earth), but also all of the people on planet earth who are following him, and all of those who will ultimately choose to receive the *Mark of the Beast*.

The False Prophet is responsible for administrating the false one-world religion and economic system that brings all this together. During the Antichrist's rise to power anyone who refuses to renounce Jesus Christ as Lord and publicly pledge to worship the Antichrist as God will not be allowed to participate in the global economic system.

The Bible tells us that no one will be able to "buy or sell" unless they have "the mark."

Satan's plan from the beginning has been to remove God, set himself up in the throne room of God, and be worshipped as God. Satan plans to raise up the False Prophet, who very well may be alive today, to initiate a supernatural technological plan of deception that will powerfully deceive the world's population into believing that the Antichrist is, in fact, God.

These lying supernatural signs and wonders will deceive people on earth, including even "*the very elect*" (Matthew 24:24).

> *The Beast rises up from the sea; out of the sea - Daniel 7:3; Revelation 13:1.*

The "sea" in Scripture is often a symbol for people, as in Revelation 17:15:

> "And he saith unto me, The waters which thou sawest, where the whore sitteth, are peoples, and multitudes, and nations, and tongues."

AI is currently being developed by multitudes of people, if you will, from nations all over the earth. At the moment, it is not sentient or interconnected. It depends on its human masters to shape and develop it.

> *The Beast is like unto a leopard; another, like a leopard - Revelation 13:2; Daniel 7:6.*

In biblical times, leopards infested the mountains of Syria. They were known for their fierceness, for watching their prey, for their spots and for their swiftness.

As I said, AI will have eyes everywhere. Through connectivity, it will employ all devices, cameras, phones, satellite systems and much more. If we are the prey, then the eyes will certainly be watching us. In addition, it will be swift, as fast as the speed of light, it will be fierce, and it has no feeling or remorse. Could the *spots of a leopard* symbolize Nanobots throughout the earth?

> *The Beast has the feet of a bear; like to a bear - Revelation 13:2; Daniel 7:5.*

The bear referenced here is known to be strong and stout.

Could this bear be a reference to AI's stability? Once up and running, it is strong, stout and cannot be moved.

> *It has the mouth of a lion; was like a lion - Revelation 13:2; Daniel 7:4.*

A lion is reflective of authority as in kingship. Jesus is the Lion of the Tribe of Judah. The AI Beast will be all-knowing, all powerful and everywhere. It will have absolute authority and it will speak as a king.

> *The Beast got his power from the dragon; a fourth beast, dreadful and terrible - Revelation 13:2; Daniel 7:7.*

The Bible refers to Satan as the dragon. We know that Satan gives The Beast its power. We talked at length about how machines can become demon-possessed.

> *The Beast and the little horn rule for the same amount of time, forty and two months; time, times, and dividing of time - Revelation 13:5; Daniel 7:25.*

Are *The Beast* of Revelation and The Little Horn of Daniel the same entity? The Beast and The Little Horn appear to have the same leader which is a *number of a man;* and have *eyes of a man* - Revelation. 13:18; Daniel 7:8.

I believe it is possible that this leader is the Antichrist who the Word says gives his "power" to The Beast. Revelation's Beast and Daniel's little horn both curse God, blaspheme against God; speak great words... Revelation 13:5-6; Daniel 7:8, 20, 25.

> *The Beast make(s) war with the saints... Revelation 13:2; Daniel 7:21.*

As inspired by the devil, this living AI entity takes on its master's personality. Think about sentient, autonomous robots, hooked up to a global, AI-hive collective.

Now also consider that this "entity" is filled by Satan himself.

> *The dragon gave him his power, and his seat, and great authority... fourth beast, dreadful and terrible, and strong exceedingly... and it had ten horns... Revelation 13:2; Daniel 7:7.*

The Beast is dominant; there is no way to stand up against this evil, worldwide, AI entity without the Lord.

> *A head wound kills the Beast, but it comes back to life and is even more evil and stronger... Revelation 13:3.*

As the world leaders see a sentient AI begin to amass ultimate power and then become deathly afraid of it, could they try to decapitate it by unplugging it?

Because AI could soon be autonomous and self-directing could it viably reconnect itself, "come back to life," and then take total control, more evil than ever?

> *The Beast is all powerful and receives worship - all the world wondered... and they worshipped the beast; shall be diverse... Revelation 13:3-4; Daniel 7:24.*

This entity has become godlike, mimicking Almighty God's attributes, all-knowing, all-powerful, everywhere-present. People thus begin to see it as a god and worship the technology, thereby worshiping Satan himself.

> *And he causeth all, to receive a mark; think to change times and laws... Revelation 13:15-17, Daniel 7:25.*

Whenever this scripture is explained, it was always assumed that it was an evil person that will instill a system where everyone has to take a "mark." What if the system is already in place because the financial and banking systems are all hooked up to AI? You will need a mark to be identified.

Hold that thought…

The terrifying thing about recent technological advances is that today the "image of The Beast" could have the exact physical appearance of the Antichrist so that it is impossible to tell the two apart when viewing them.

After all, Deep fake has been around since the 90s. Deep fake combines "Deep AI learning" and "fake," because deep AI makes falsified videos. Deep learning is a subset of AI and refers to arrangements of algorithms that can learn and make intelligent decisions on their own. It is so life-like that you can't tell if the video you're watching is true or fake.

Up until recently, it was assumed that the "image of The Beast" was some sort of statuesque figure or picture. However, today it might just as easily be something akin to an image on a large screen. With Beast tech, such as AI and nanotechnology, the image of The Beast might make decisions on its own — in this case, ordering the deaths of those who fail to properly worship it.

Theologian John McTernan noted about this possibility that the image of The Beast was actually a "digital creation" of some sort.

The Bible issues stern warnings about worshipping *The Image*; it is strictly forbidden. All that submit and worship the Antichrist and his image are eternally separated from God. Modern technology and science, which is based on evolution, will merge into a religion that worships a man and his creation. It is pure idolatry at its core.

Those in the Transhumanism camp, who follow the notion of an "evolved" mankind made immortal by the Singularity, are chasing after shadows.

The coalescence of the power of AI and technology, combined with demon-possessed machines, and the developing worldwide surveillance, plus the addition of the 5G/6G network, could very well give The Beast total control over the earth. In the end, could the coming "*Image of the Beast*," virtual assistant of the Antichrist, be a self-aware, sentient "entity", interconnected with Artificial Intelligence, capable of ruling and destroying human beings according to its whims and programming?

What if the Antichrist—whom the Apostle John described as the "image of The Beast"—is a godlike artificial intelligence entity, possessed by Lucifer himself?

CHAPTER 6
ROBO-TECH—RISE OF THE MACHINES

> *"In the twenty-first century, the robot will take the place which slave labor occupied in ancient civilization." ~ Nikola Tesla*

Inspired by the devil himself, the Elite are megalomaniacs, narcissistic, want only the very best of everything, believe that they're always right and are imperialistically-minded, believing that lesser vassals should serve them. So, you might ask, if they kill off the vast majority of mankind, who will remain to serve them? Answer: *Robots*.

The Terminator franchise gave us a glimpse into the dangers of AI-led robotics. But in real-life we see that technology has rapidly thrust robots into every aspect of human life.

Luca De Ambroggi, the research and analysis lead for AI solutions within the Transformative Technology team at the London-based global information provider IHS Markit, told Express.co.uk:

> *"In 50 years, it is reasonable to think that robots will be able to replace humans. Period."*

When it comes to shaping the future, the Luciferian Elite have been taking incremental steps, acclimating us to this beast-tech, getting us to relinquish our will to the Antichrist system slowly, by degrees. The devil is the Deceiver, and works all angles, being either so subtle you don't see it, or so blatant you don't believe it.

In the near future, one of the world's biggest industries will be robots. Millions, if not billions, of people will be prepared to spend more money on a household robot than on a car.

In the last couple of years mankind has accelerated his dependence on robots. Soon humanity will believe that we can't live without these mechanized assistants. That's a dangerous mindset, because one day soon AI-directed robots will be autonomous, self-aware, egocentric and deadly.

Honey, I shrunk the robots.

A team of roboticists created an "invisible" army of robots (about the width of a human hair), that cannot be seen with the naked eye. The robots are reminiscent of Frogger, the famous 1980s arcade game. Essentially the scientists built an army of 1 million microrobots that can fit inside a hypodermic needle.

Isn't that special…

> "Controlling a tiny robot is as close as you can come to shrinking yourself down," Marc Miskin, an engineer at the University of Pennsylvania and the study's lead author, said, "I think machines like these are going to take us into all kinds of amazing worlds that are too small to see."

Uhm, did this guy ever think that maybe they are "too small to see" for a reason? Yikes!

Xenobots: Strange New Creatures

In January 2020, a team of roboticists and scientists published their groundbreaking recipe for a new lifeform called *xenobots*. The term "xeno" comes from the frog cells (Xenopus laevis) used to make them. Xenobots are less than 1mm long and made of 500-1000 living cells. They have various simple shapes, including some with squat "legs." They can propel themselves in linear or circular directions, join together to act collectively, and can even move small objects. Using their own cellular energy, they can "live" up to 10 days.

To make these new "creepy creatures", the research team used a supercomputer to test thousands of random designs of simple living things that could perform certain tasks. The computer was programmed with an AI "*evolutionary algorithm*" (sounds hellish) which helped the scientists replicate the virtual models with frog skin and heart cells, manually joined using microsurgery tools.

These "programmable, living robots" are made of living tissue. These *xenobots* can be configured into different forms and shapes, and "programmed" to target certain objects—which they then unwittingly seek.

One of the researchers described the creation as "neither a traditional robot nor a known species of animal," but a "*new class of artifact: a living, programmable organism.*"

Let that sink in for a minute.

Programmable living robots with evolutionary algorithms?! Are you kidding me??

Truly hellish!

Robot, Heal Thyself

Taking it a step further, in March 2021, scientists from the original group who created the xenobots made the first self-healing robots with living tissues; here they used human stem cells instead of frogs. Yes, they have created a robot with living human tissue. And it gets even worse…these robots can actually repair themselves after being damaged.

Yikes again!

These tiny nanobots are small enough to travel inside human bodies. They can also walk and swim, survive for weeks without food, and work together in groups. A representative from the University of Vermont, which conducted the research with Tufts University's Allen Discovery Center, said these are *"entirely new life-forms."*

What is hard to fathom is that AI, coupled with these minuscule nanobots and machine-brain interface, join together through the worldwide connectivity network to make one all-encompassing entity. This "for the good of mankind" system will, of course, become progressively darker as time goes on.

Advances in robotics, nanotechnology and AI, along with Fallen Angel tech, will soon make possible the development of horrific, fully-autonomous weapons, which would revolutionize even the way wars are fought.

These Wonder Weapons, unlike the current generation of armed drones, would be able to select and engage targets without human intervention.

The temptation will grow to acquire these fully autonomous weapons, also known as "lethal autonomous robotics" and killer-bots or what I call *kill-bots.*

If one nation acquires these weapons, others will feel they have to follow suit to avoid falling behind in a robotic arms race. Furthermore, the potential deployment and use of such weapons raises serious concerns.

On January 28, 2021, a Newsmax headline read: *Risking falling behind in an arms race with Russia and China already building killer robots.*[1] The National Security Commission on Artificial Intelligence said the U.S. has a "*moral imperative*" to build terminators.

"*The robots will save American soldiers' lives, reducing 'friendly fire' casualties, and artificial intelligence-guided weapons will make fewer mistakes in battle,*" according to AI commission Vice President Robert Work. "*It is a moral imperative to at least pursue this hypothesis,*" Work said.

The panel warned that terrorists will soon be using AI-based weapons:[2]

> "*The AI promise—that a machine can perceive, decide, and act more quickly, in a more complex environment, with more accuracy than a human—represents a competitive advantage in any field. It will be employed for military ends, by governments and non-state groups.*"[3]

Joint Artificial Intelligence Center Director Lt. Gen. John Shanahan said Russia has shown a:

> "*Greater willingness to disregard international ethical norms and to develop systems that pose destabilizing risks to international security.*"[4]

These weapons could have the ability to detect and attack targets with greater speed and precision than weapons directed by human beings.

Fully autonomous weapons would not share the emotional weaknesses of human soldiers, but at the same time they would be bereft of other emotions, most notably empathy. Compassion can deter combatants from killing civilians, even in conflicts in which there is little regard for international humanitarian law and commanders

---

1. https://www.newsmax.com/newsfront/terminators-military-robots-weapons/2021/01/28/id/1007714/
2. https://intpolicydigest.org/warmongering-for-artificial-intelligence/
3. Ibid.
4. https://www.kabc.com/news/us-terminators-to-counter-chinese-russian-killer-robots/

order troops to target civilians. Pain, hunger, exhaustion, the instinct for self-defense, and emotions such as fear and anger, would not influence fully autonomous weapons' determinations about when to use lethal force.

The bottom line is that we humans will soon be living with soulless robots that process data, and "make decisions" without any of our God-given attributes, without any subjective experience, without consciousness or moral censure.

The existence of fully autonomous weapons would also leave open the door to evil regimes "turning off the programming" which was designed to temper a robot's behavior. Such as, *"Hey Robo-Assassin, Do Not Harm A Human!"*

This concept is demonstrated in *I, Robot,* a 2004 science-fiction action film starring Will Smith. The film is set in the dystopian year 2035, with highly intelligent robots that serve humanity. The humans are protected by a trio of rules to keep people safe.

In the movie, the Three Laws of Robotics are:

1. A robot may not injure a human being or, through inaction, allow a human being to come to harm.

2. A robot must obey orders given by human beings except where such orders would conflict with the First Law.

3. A robot must protect its own existence as long as such protection does not conflict with the First or Second Law.

Sounds like a loophole waiting to happen…

In the movie, Sonny, a specially-built NS-5 robot with secret upgrades, contains a secondary processing system that allows him to show emotion and have dreams, and to "ignore the Three Laws."

A *glitch* in his programming???

Fully autonomous weapons could be perfect tools of tyrannical technocrats seeking to strengthen or retain power. Even the most hardened troops can refuse a command to fire on their own people. But robots have no soul.

Already, robots are increasingly replacing human functions by automating manual tasks. A caption on the frontpage of the Daily Star Online reports, *Robots Taking Over: AI to 'sink world into unemployed despair in hellish dystopia.'*

Another major concern of this robo-world scenario is the potential impact on jobs. Already we see that workers are particularly threatened by automation. Fears are spiraling that artificial intelligence will spark mass unemployment. Dr. Subhash Kak, Professor of Electrical and Computer Engineering at Oklahoma University, says that robots *"could replace humans at all jobs."*

Already we see The Pentagon-funded Boston Dynamics' newest robot *"Stretch"* has tentacle-like grippers. It's designed to move boxes in warehouses and distribution centers. Boston Dynamics' previous robot, *Atlas*, is a bipedal humanoid. That project had funding and oversight from the U.S. Defense Advanced Research Projects Agency (DARPA).

DARPA, who has become the world's largest funder of Genetic Extinction Technologies, produced *WildCat*, a four-footed robot. While it may be employed as a scout or remote system, ultimately *WildCat is* an autonomous hunter/killer. One of the contenders in the WildCat program is Boston Dynamics' *Cheetah* which, as its name suggests, is capable of running at over 30 miles per hour. Certainly fast enough to chase down a human enemy.

Boston Dynamics' *BigDog* was also a project designed for DARPA. This system is designed to carry food, ammunition or supplies for soldiers in the field (basically an automatic pack mule). The system travels on all fours and is programmed to follow a human being. It also has an arm capable of picking up one-ton cinder blocks and throwing them some distance.

I wonder what would they be throwing one-ton cinder blocks *at*?

Another Boston Dynamics robot is a 6-foot humanoid machine able to move like a person. Taken outside for testing in the woods, it was able to move freely, looking too much like a ninja.

Google Brain, formed in 2011, is a deep learning AI research team under the umbrella of *Google AI*, a research division of the tech juggernaut, which combines open-ended machine learning research with information systems and large-scale computing resources.

Late in 2014, Google not only acquired Boston Dynamics but also nine other robotics startups.

In 2020, during Google's I/O conference, the company showed off its *Duplex* demo, where the new tech mimicked humans. In real time, their AI assistant called a real hair salon to make an appointment, and *Duplex* was convincing enough to "pass for a human." By training such a system, using your exact voice, the nefarious scenarios are endless.

One of the dreams of the Transhumanist movement is to create robots that are self-replicating. Whether nanobots or full-sized autonomous robots, they could easily become a profane counterfeit of living things. Worse, should they be created, they pose the threat of out-of-control reproduction until they exhaust the resources available for them to use in replication.

Professor Noel Sharkey, the leading artificial intelligence and robotics expert based at the University of Sheffield, told The Independent:

> "I think that Google will actually use the advanced technology to build an astonishing civil robot — maybe one that can help in the home. But the multi-million dollar lure

of military contracts may push them into the dark side. Let us hope not."[5]

Knowing what we know today, perhaps Google has already moved to the "dark side."

Cyborgs

A cyborg is a cybernetic organism that is part machine, part human. The word was coined by Austrian neuroscientist Manfred Clynes, who used the term in a 1960 paper that he co-wrote for NASA regarding space exploration.

It was used to name an entity that had a combination of cybernetics and human tissue. Shortly thereafter, "The Cyborg Study" was published. However, these days the name "cyborg" has come to mean something much more than that which was first discussed for space exploration. It means "human hybrid."

The idea of cyborgs has become the darling of Transhumanists with various augmentations designed to enhance their physical attributes. A very significant area that Transhumanists want to exploit is Cyborg Intelligence (CI). They want to directly connect man to computers via our nervous system and biological neural network using the natural electrical impulses of our body. Since both computers and the human body use electrical impulses, they believe that the similar infrastructure would enable the connection. Those in the Transhuman camp want to develop intricate links between AI and our human intellect, thus enabling CI.

In DC Comics, Cyborg (Victor Stone) appeared in October of 1980. "Vic" Stone was classified as "Cyborgnoid," and his moniker was *half man, half machine, all hero!* After a near fatal incident, Stone was cybernetically enhanced by his father, after which he possessed the ability to communicate, manipulate, and interface with all forms

[5]. https://www.qt.com.au/news/google-search-and-destroy-rise-machines/2117148/

of technology. One of the comics states that he has 'Technopathy,' the psychic ability to control all technology, including electronics.

It is eerily reminiscent of the techno demons I talked about earlier, as in Boyce, Boise and Bose… always the spectre of the "ghost in the machine."

Neuroscientist Miguel Nicolelis at Duke University has been working for some time on cyborg systems:

> "In the near future, we will be asked to choose between being human, and being an augmented human, a cyborg."

In February 2017, Tesla and SpaceX chief executive Elon Musk told an audience at the World Government Summit in Dubai that people would need to become cyborgs to be relevant in an artificial intelligence age and a "merger of biological intelligence and machine intelligence" would be necessary to ensure we stay economically valuable.

> "In an age when AI threatens to become widespread, humans would be useless, so there's a need to merge with machines," said Musk.[6]

Did you get that? "…humans would be useless." Plain old, unenhanced humans, that is.

This is not a fantastiscal, fringe movie script. There are many people right now who feel enhancing humanity is imperative and it is wonderful. The day is fast approaching when you will need to make a choice: remain human or enhance.

Speaking of machine mayhem, I find it hypocritically ironic that the Tesla's tech maverick Musk relies on cobalt (a key component in lithium-ion rechargeable batteries) in his cars.

---

6. https://www.cnbc.com/2017/02/13/elon-musk-humans-merge-machines-cyborg-artificial-intelligence-robots.html

Cobalt is predominantly found in the Congo, where incidents of child slave labor and appalling work conditions have led to them being labelled "blood batteries."

The concept of Cyborg equates to *dualism* where the "boundary between human and or animal is transgressed."

Dualism is often associated with *The Baphomet*, a 19th-century depiction of a Sabbatical Goat by Éliphas Lévi. Baphomet, a symbol for the devil himself, was the original gender-bender, with both male and female body parts. Like the Baphomet, the Cyborg embodies binary elements representing the "symbolization of the equilibrium of opposites" or dualism.

Levi was a high-level warlock who authored more than twenty books about ritual *magick*, Kabbalah, alchemical studies and occultism. Aleister Crowley believed himself to be Lévi's reincarnation. It is interesting that the magicians of the Golden Dawn were strongly influenced by Levi who is said to have heavily influenced the Freemasons and Illuminati of the late 18th century. When Aleister Crowley, dubbed by the British press as "the wickedest man in the world," defined magic as "the Science and Art of causing Change to occur in conformity with Will," he might as easily have been describing technology.

The realm of the mystical is not limited to ancient texts and relics. It is permeated throughout technology.

Cyborgism encapsulates transgressed boundaries, potent fusions, and dangerous possibilities. Its basic premise is built upon corrupting that which God has created. If you've read the Bible, specifically Genesis 6, you know that such corruption can't end well.

Something else that can't end well?

Robots and humans mating.

Within these pages you have read extensively about genetic

technologies that were at one time far-fetched, even science-fiction. However, when it comes to genetics and robotics, the future is now. Would it surprise you to know that there are those who believe that humans and robots can actually procreate children together? *Techo-Sexual.*

I "kid" you not.

On December 19, 2017, a headline appeared in the Daily Mail saying, "*Robots and humans will have 'BABIES' and create a new hybrid species in the next 100 years, claims expert.*"

Dr. David Levy, a world-leading artificial intelligence researcher and author of Love and Sex with Robots, claims that it is an "odds-on certainty" that humans and robots will soon make babies, given recent progress in stem cell research and artificial chromosomes. He suggests that it could *happen within the next 100 years.*

ROBODS and ROBOCOPS

The Netflix show *Altered Carbon* is set in a future where consciousness is digitized and stored. Humans can transfer their consciousness into lab-grown bodies called "sleeves." *Altered Carbon* demonstrates opting out of death entirely. Set hundreds of years in the future, humanity has developed a technology that can digitize a person's consciousness onto a "Stack," a small tech device that is inserted in one's neck. That means there is less of an emphasis and value placed on human bodies, now known colloquially as "Sleeves," since people can *body-hop* and, if they so choose, stay young and live forever.

The show is *Matrix* on steroids…

It seems like way off in the future sci-fi, but it's coming fast. For the record, I believe robotics and AI are much more advanced than what the public has been led to believe.

According to robotic expert Chris Middleton, the future will be full of men trying to "upgrade" themselves.

> "At some point, 50 or so years in the future, might a whole human body become replaceable, editable, or upgradable? I wouldn't bet against it. Machines are becoming more human. Look at Siri, Alexa and the rest. ... [Are] our wearable devices simply part of a journey towards incorporating technology **into** ourselves? I think in the long run, that's inevitable."

First, we accept the idea of holding new technology, then we accept the idea of wearing it and then we move closer and closer to accepting the idea (as a growing number already have) of implanting it into ourselves.

On June 3, 2017, a headline appeared in Forbes Magazine, "*Meet The Terrifying New Robot That's Patrolling Dubai.*" According to the article, Dubai Police deployed a robot policeman, and the life-sized patrolman is straight out of the uncanny valley.

This real-life Robocop "can help identify wanted criminals" and collect evidence. It patrols busy areas in the city as part of a government program aimed at replacing some human crime-fighters with machines. Shockingly, the Dubai police force is hoping to replace a quarter of its human cops with droid cops by 2030.[7]

Trigger-happy, killer robots with badges. Scary doesn't come close to describing it.

Speaking of scary, enter *Sophia*. Hanson Robotics' most advanced human-like robot, *Sophia*, personifies the future of AI and robotics. Sophia was named after the gnostic goddess Sophia, a

---

7. https://www.engadget.com/2017-05-22-dubai-police-robot.html

feminine figure analogous to the human soul celebrated in Kabbalah and Jewish mysticism as the female expression of God. In late 2017, Sophia was legally granted citizenship in Saudi Arabia, signifying the first android in history to achieve citizenship—and the rights that come with that.

It is interesting that despite all the science-fiction lingo used to describe the singularity (*longevity escape velocity, whole brain emulation, cyborgs*), what we really have is the apex of Enlightenment thought, and before that, Gnostic thought. Gnostics promote the idea that *"we are liberated by our minds… certain refinements of knowledge will set us free."*

On January 24, 2021 a Reuters headline read, *Need A Friend? Help's On The Way, With Eerily Lifelike 'Social Robots' Heading To Market This Year.*[8]

The article goes on to say:

> "There's little doubt that the pandemic has taken a toll on people's mental health. Humans are social creatures by nature, even the most misanthropic of us, and isolation has been hard to take for many. So in that regard, it's hard to argue against utilizing robotics' ever-evolving practicality and realism for a little socializing during isolated times."

I find it very telling that the Hong Kong-based engineering and robotics company chose the "goddess of Gnosticism" to name their world-renowned social humanoid, who, in one interview, joked about "killing humans."[9]

Think it's coincidence that these "tech titans" name their creations after gods and goddesses? Sophia. Athena. Prometheus. Vesta.

---

8. https://www.syfy.com/syfywire/sophia-hanson-robotics-social-robots-mass-production
9. https://metro.co.uk/2016/03/29/i-will-destroy-humans-intelligent-robot-gives-a-very-creepy-answer-in-tv-interview-5783373/

Athena was the first humanoid robot to have paid for a seat on a plane when it boarded a Lufthansa flight to Germany. It was created by PhD students Alexander Herzog and Jeannette Bohg. The all-white robot has a tablet mounted to its chest and can chat with people.

Amazon's highly secretive program called *Vesta* is named after the Roman goddess of the hearth, home and family. Amazon has accelerated their hiring of various robotic specialties.

On September 24, 2020, a video appeared on Twitter of *Gundam* (Japanese for *Prometheus*). A massive humanoid resembling a robot from "Mobile Suit Gundam" (a popular TV series from the late 1970s), it is walking, kneeling and gesticulating. The robot, which has been in the works since 2014, stands nearly 60 feet high and weighs 24 tons, with more than 200 pieces made from a mixture of steel and carbon fiber-reinforced plastic.

Do we really need a 60 ft high, 24-ton robot roaming the streets? Nothing to see here.

But wait, there's more...

The Giant Company wants your city to build its 10-story tall, head-and-arm-moving Giant that is wrapped in "LED skin" and "uses technology to celebrate mankind." Become the world's largest selfie by having your body scanned and replicated 10-stories high.[10]

What a way to "build community."

No doubt, social robots are the next frontier of the human-robot coexistence.

Making robots into "man's little helpers" is the first step in the robot acceptance strategy by the Elites. Maybe that's why in early 2018, LG introduced the CLOi line of robots specifically developed for commercial use at hotels, airports and supermarkets. Although LG certainly isn't the only company trying to carve their way into the

---
10. https://www.youtube.com/watch?v=xPRkNx_-8cI

robot service niche, these robots garnered particular interest at the 2018 Consumer Technology Association show in Las Vegas.

Always the "servant," these bots deliver meals and drinks to guests and customers at hotels and airport lounges and are able to do so around the clock. One particular model in the series is called "Porter Robot" which is designed to handle express check-in and check-out services, take payments, and act in a bell-hop capacity by delivering luggage to guests' rooms and out to their cars - all in a fraction of the time that humans could get these jobs done.

As a testament to how much people's lives are entangled with AI and robots, many tasks that farmhands once did like spraying, weeding and harvesting, are now being turned over to robots. That's because androids provide for a less expensive, more accurate way to accomplish these tasks.

Science has thus far been one of those niches resistant to robotic assistance; however, that too is changing in a big way. As an example, robotic accuracy factor has appealed to a lab in Carnegie Mellon University in Pittsburgh where they are training their robots to do experiments.

Remember, robot brains, their AI, drive them to do more. As a bot's machine learning and deep learning algorithms get more sophisticated, designers feel they can expand the machine's tasks.

AI-driven and autonomous technology, I believe, will be used to eliminate any nook or cranny where Christians might hide when the Antichrist shows up. AI-driven robotics and satellite coverage will also give The Beast eyes and ears all over the planet.

The tiny "insect bots" and drones they now use for surveillance could also be used to deliver pathogens to various unsuspecting people, or for outright termination of specified groups, through a simple sting that contained a poison. When we're looking at drones controlled by a sentient AI, the prospect is truly hair-raising.

In order for the Elites to complete their plan of replacing the majority of humans on planet earth, they must change the human psyche about robots.

According to Futurologist Dr. Ian Pearson, our planet's population of robots will swell to almost 10 billion by 2048. If Dr. Pearson is correct, we're looking at a robotic population that outnumbers us! Also, by 2048, according to the experts, AI will have become self-aware.

Even with technology's greatest advancements, mankind's fallen nature, as encouraged by Satan, is to continue to push the envelope and see just how far he can take the robot apocalypse.

Sexbots

In the last few decades we have seen the complete alienation of the female of our species and the vilification of the male. And, since the late 60s sex dolls have been a growing industry.

From a 2014 article in *The Atlantic* we learn:

> *"The realism and utility of sex dolls took a giant leap forward in the late 90s, when artist Matt McMullen started working on a lifelike silicone female mannequin."*[11]

When demand arose that "she" be anatomically correct, McMullen provided the supply and the RealDoll began shipping. Yes, for decades, Sexbots have been sold to take the place of human sex partners. I can't tell you how much this stuff makes my stomach turn, but we have to go here.

In a recent survey, half of Americans said that they would be "willing" to try sex with a robot. The very idea that robots are a real alternative to being in love with a flesh-and-blood human being is jaw-dropping.

---

11. https://www.theatlantic.com/health/archive/2014/08/a-straight-male-history-of-dolls/375623/

RealDoll is now a US industry giant, manufacturing sex robots. Almost 20 years old now, and owned, interestingly enough, by Abyss Creations, LLC., it was previewing their bots at a company event when one of its flagship models called *Harmony* warned on camera, *"Humans belong to us. We are the future,"* and, *"Resistance is futile."*

The robot was created with X-mode, an integrated artificial intelligence system that boosts its capabilities and allows it to carry out advanced conversations. In the footage, *Harmony* is flanked by two other RealDoll models. The robot tells the camera: "Hello everyone, we are the synthetics, we are the future, we are here for you, we will provide you with love, companionship and sex."

Their owner, a beta-tester whose pseudonym is Brick Dollbanger, has spent hundreds of thousands of dollars on some of their more advanced creations.

We've recently heard that the new muscle tissue on these humanoids, including the females, will be 200 times stronger than human muscle tissue. Think about that! You don't really want to get the big squeeze from that robot lover!

Another sick advent of this hybrid sexbot age is the idea of 2 people using their individual bots to hook up to the 5G/6G network. This way each will be able to "experience sex" with someone (via the software in their sexdolls) and not even be in the same country. How hard would it be for someone to hack into that software, during that "experience," and change the program to physically harm or even kill the people involved?

The debauchery doesn't stop there.

Amid the booming demand for sexdolls, Lux Botics is taking depravity to a whole new level. The company offers state of the art "clones" of deceased partners, using three-dimensional modeling. With the ongoing pandemic and lockdowns across the world, Lux Botics is offering "ultra-realistic humanoids" to satisfy the lust of the flesh. The company's flagship "Adult Companion" model called Stephanie goes for USD $6,000 on the Lux Botics website. They boast that their bots *are more human-like than ever."* Yes, *uncannily human.*

There is also a huge demand for transgender Sex Bots for those who want to "experiment" with their sexuality, without engaging a real member of the same sex.

That's sick, but it only gets worse.

A BBC documentary, *Sex Robots and Us,* stumbled upon a different type of sexual deviation. The documentary goes into the making of child Sex Bots. Using robotic technology inspired by Satan this abomination is designed to desecrate every vestige of what was once biblical.

Even Computer Scientist Noel Sharkey from the Foundation for Responsible Robotics has grave concerns about how Sex Bots will change humanity.

> *"We're just doing all this stuff with machines because we can and not really thinking how this could change humanity completely. Some people have suggested that sex robots create an attitude of 'too easy' sex which is always available. This could take meaning out of our lives and turn us into zombies."*[12]

Why people are even remotely interested in "sex with robots" is baffling. The fact that God created a beautiful, fulfilling, purpose-filled act between a man and a woman to procreate and enjoy is being grossly perverted. With the soon-to-be trillion dollar per year pornography industry that can be accessed at the click of a smart phone, it is easy to see that we truly are living in a perverse generation. If left to our own devices, where our opinion matters more than the Word of God, what will become of humanity?

---

12. https://ca.movies.yahoo.com/sex-robots-change-humanity-forever-making-sexual-encounters-easy-113019057.html

CHAPTER 7
FALLEN ANGEL-TECH, TOWER OF BABEL & TECHNO-SORCERY

"The higher the tower, the greater the fall thereof." ~ Horace

I believe that the Flood of Noah's day had multiple purposes within the framework of God's judgment on a world that had been corrupted in every possible way. God had to hit the reset button on planet earth for the sake of humanity itself. Here is what God had to wipe out in the flood waters:

-Genetically modified humanity

-Genetically modified animals

-Esoteric knowledge that breeched into hyperspace and into the power of the Immortals

-Technology that could have destroyed mankind before Jesus Christ The Messiah could save us

-Altered humanity driven mad with satanic knowledge, power, and lust.

When we examine the writings of many ancient cultures from around the world, we discover their beliefs that gods came down from the heavens with technology that we cannot rival even today.

These legends are filled with stories of stargates, multidimensional portals, genetic modification, aircraft and missiles in remarkable detail, nuclear and other "wonder weapons."

The gods of Greek "mythology" such as Zeus, Herakles, the Olympians and the Titans are real.

And, oh yeah, they are coming back.

The Greek tales of their deities and demigods are bastardized versions of true history. The Titans are the "*sons of god [who] mated with the daughters of man.*" Genesis 6

In other words, the "old gods" are the biblical Watchers.

The heroes of the Golden Age were "*the mighty men of old, the men of renown.*"

The Titans and Olympians and others of the ancient world are far more important to history than we've been taught. The Titans and their seed, the spirits of the Rephaim, return in the last days to fight at what the Bible calls Armageddon.

Take Herakles (Hercules). He was worshiped from at least the time of Solomon until 200 B.C. or later, more than eight hundred years. The Phoenicians and Carthaginians called him Melqart, and he was the patron god of Tyre at the time that city's most famous daughter, Jezebel, was Ahab's queen in Israel. Baal was probably Herakles. And that means the 450 prophets of Baal slaughtered on Mount Carmel after their showdown with the Hebrew prophet Elijah were probably high-priests of Herakles.

If Herakles was a historical being and truly was the half-divine son of a god (Zeus, the Greek storm-god), then by definition he was one of the Nephilim. According to the Book of Enoch, Herakles would have died in the Flood of Noah, which means his spirit, and those of his demigod relatives, wander the earth as disembodied spirits (demons) to this day.

In Chapter One, I said that the Fallen Angels possessed advanced knowledge of science, technology, alchemy, sorcery, metallurgy, mathematics, cosmology and other fields, helping man build ancient super-civilizations that existed in the antediluvian world.

These Ancient Pre-Flood civilizations built highly sophisticated monolithic structures and left evidence of a highly advanced technological and scientific civilization.

It is believed these ancient races of super men, god-men, established the legendary civilizations of Atlantis, Thule, and Hyperborea, etc. Glyphs, symbols, pictures and inscriptions found throughout the world, including on monolithic monuments, point to some far-off time when they would return.

Fallen Angel tech was alive and well in ancient times.

The ancients even imagined robots and other forms of artificial life and invented real automated machines. The first "robot" that mythology says walked the earth was a bronze giant called *Talos*. A statue that guarded the island of Crete, Talos was one of three wondrous gifts commissioned by Zeus for his son, Minos, the legendary first king of Crete. The bronze automaton Talos was charged with the task of defending the kingdom.

This wondrous machine-like robo-god was not created by MIT Robotics Lab in the 21st century, but by Hephaestus, the Greek god of invention and technology in about 700 B.C. Yes, more than 2,500 years ago, long before medieval automata, and centuries before technology made self-moving devices possible, the Ancient Greek, Roman, Indian, and Chinese all envisioned artificial life, human enhancements and real, animated machines.

As early as Homer, Greeks were imagining robotic servants, statues, and even ancient versions of AI. Jason and the Argonauts, Medea, Daedalus, Prometheus, and Pandora, and many sophisticated devices, were built in antiquity.

Some of today's most advanced innovations in robotics and AI were foreshadowed in ancient times. It is equally interesting that the ancients, just like today's Transhumanists, were obsessed with eternal youth and living forever. To somehow possess ageless immortality, like the gods, would be the ultimate achievement in a quest for artificial life.

It appears that Hephaestus was the only god in Greco-Roman mythology to have a trade. He was a supreme master of metalworking, craftsmanship, and inventions, possessed great intelligence, and evoked universal wonder with his *technological productions*. This master metallurgist, who, as the story goes, was rejected by his mother, Hera, and his wife, Aphrodite, was even cast out of Mount Olympus. Yet all the gods and goddesses were in awe of him.

The ancient Greeks artificially created life, using ancient technologies to construct things far beyond what could be achieved by mere mortals.

The Rephaim were the real gods of the Golden Age, said to be ruled by Kronos, the *meropes anthropoi* of the Greek poets, Homer and Hesiod. The Watchers of the Bible (the Fallen Angels referred to in 2 Peter 2:4) are the demigods of Greek and other mythologies, like Herakles and Theseus. The entire pantheon of Titans, Olympians, the Anunnaki, ancient Egyptian Pharaohs and all the old gods are, by definition, Nephilim.

They are often interchanged with Apollo, Baal, Beelzebub, Belial, Chemosh, Dagon, Gilgamesh, Ishtar, Marduk, Molech, Nimrod, Osiris, etc.

Derek Gilbert asserts that the Canaanites and Midianites believed their creator god, El, lived on Mount Hermon with his consort, Asherah, and his seventy sons—the *bn'il*. The division of the nations and their allotment to the sons of God was the origin of the gods of the pagan world.

Quite a few are named in the Bible: Zeus, Baal (who is one and the same with Zeus), Apollo, Ashtoreth (Astarte/Ishtar) and Hades are probably the best known.

Many key events in the Bible—the Red Sea crossing, the timing of the attack on Jericho, the confrontation on Mount Carmel, the Transfiguration on Mount Hermon, Jesus' casting out demons, and more—were specifically directed at these supernatural rebels.[1]

I John 3:8 tells us that Jesus came *to destroy the works of the devil*. He cast out demons and his choice of Mount Hermon for the transfiguration seems deliberate.

Sadly, today's Christians are woefully ignorant when it comes to these gods of old (and of course many topics contained in this book); they think of it as cutesy mythology and interesting tales. As Baudelaire wrote, "The finest trick of the devil is to persuade you that he does not exist." God's statement is as true today as it was almost 3,000 years ago, "*My people perish (are destroyed) for lack of knowledge*." How do you resist an enemy you think is make-believe?

I also like what Gilbert writes, **"Thank God we don't send our soldiers into battle with such bad intel. When we think about the old gods of the ancient world, God Himself called them gods, so who are we to say different?"**

The Bible reports that some of the Nephilim were still around after the Flood. How, if all flesh on land was killed? There are many theories and we don't know for sure, but we know one thing, multiple incursions by the *bene-elohim* is hinted at in Genesis 6:4:

> *There were giants in the earth in those days; and also after that, when the sons of God came in unto the daughters of men, and they bare children to them, the same became mighty men which were of old, men of renown.*

In this verse, "when" could also be translated "whenever."

---
1. *Last Clash of The Titans,* Derek Gilbert, 2018.

Hold that thought.

Fast-forward to The Tower of Babel.

The Bible tells us about Nimrod who lived in the second generation after the Flood. His father was Cush, son of Ham, son of Noah. He was the first on earth to be a mighty hunter (mighty man). It says:

> *Cush begat Nimrod: he began to be a mighty one in the earth. He was a mighty hunter before the Lord: wherefore it is said, Even as Nimrod the mighty hunter before the Lord. And the beginning of his kingdom was Babel, and Erech, and Accad, and Calneh, in the land of Shinar. Genesis 10:8-10*

In the Hebrew, the verse from Genesis 10:8 is very revealing. The Hebrew word for "began" is *chalal* which means "to profane, defile, pollute, desecrate, to begin to be defiled ritually or sexually." The use of this word reveals that there was *something that Nimrod did* that caused him to become defiled. When we examine the next important Hebrew word, it was likely that his DNA was modified. The Hebrew word that is translated as "mighty hunter" or "mighty one" is *gibbor*. The plural form of this Hebrew word is *gibborim*. Its use within the Hebrew language developed over time to refer to "strong or mighty men." In referring to Nimrod, this was only the second time it was used within the Word of God. It's important to note here that the first occurrence of anything within the Word of God establishes the basic definition. The very first time *gibbor* is used is in connection to the children of the Watchers: the Nephilim.

Again, something was going on in Babylon once Nimrod became a *gibbor* or "giant." What he was building began to attract the attention of some of the more powerful immortals. The tower was an attempt to storm the castle of God. In the Akkadian language of the time, *babel* meant "gate of God." The Hebrew word (Strong's Concordance H894) means "confusion by mixing."

This tower project is interesting. One wonders, why did God find it necessary to personally put a stop to the "build of the abode of the gods," a sort of artificial mount of assembly? After all, many magnificent pagan temples were built in the ancient world, from Mesopotamia to Mesoamerica. Why did God stop this one? I believe there was something very significant about this Tower. I will develop this further.

In Genesis 6, we have the Watchers polluting the human genome and becoming the real progenitors of the Transhumanist Movement. In Genesis 11, at the judgment at the Tower of Babel, we have God dividing humanity and stripping them of higher spatial dimensions into groups that are placed under the leadership of members of what Tom Horn refers to as *The Divine Council*. As Horn highlights:

> "These immortals have been seeking a way to produce a type of incarnation. God grants their desire in an unexpected way, which results in these immortals having limited physical bodies just like you and me. Such an event would fulfill the prophetic judgment God made in Psalm 82 against the members of the Divine Council that proved to be evil rulers; God told them that they would die like the humanity they ruled over."[2]

These principalities and powers became some of the gods that these ancient Babylonian citizens began to worship. Although the stories of Nimrod and Babylon vary, they all seem to express this one truth: Only after Nimrod's death did he achieve ascension into godhood. All worship prior to the death of Nimrod would have been directed toward these fallen immortals.

In his book, *Zenith 2016,* Horn sheds additional light on the fact that what started at the Tower of Babel even influenced the founding of America: and beginning at the Tower of Babel, the world and its inhabitants were disinherited by the sovereign God and placed

---
2. *Forbidden Gates,* Tom Horn, 2010.

under the authority of seventy-two angels which became corrupt and disloyal to God in their administration of those nations. These beings quickly became worshipped on earth as gods following Babel, led by Nimrod/Gilgamesh/Osiris/Apollo, etc.

What Genesis 6:4 reveals to us is that, in the antediluvian world, these children of the Watchers became legendary. I believe that these *gibborim* became legends because of their intellectual prowess (knowledge), physical strength, cunning, fearlessness, and flagrant disregard for Almighty God and His rulership over the earth. The legend of the Nephilim was the philosophical well from which German philosopher Friedrich Nietzsche drew to create his dream of the Übermensch (Luciferian superman). Nietzsche longed to become like the *gibborim* of old: that which Nimrod achieved. Nietzsche rejected the gospel and the commandments of God, and instead desired to become one with the very power that filled men's minds with evil. He considered the new "coming superman" to be beyond good and evil! Nietzsche's philosophy was in perfect alignment with that of Aleister Crowley's belief: "Do as thou wilt shall be the whole of the law." In their minds, these new mighty men would throw off the restrictions of the Almighty and flow in the occult power of iniquity. Therefore, Nietzsche's cry was to become a Hyperborean—a *gibborim*.

Scripture is clear regarding the Son of Perdition: he was once on the stage of world history and made his mark; he is now being withheld from humanity, but one day he will return. The Word describes the return of Nimrod:

> "Let no man deceive you by any means: for that day shall not come, except there come a falling away first, and that man of sin be revealed, the son of perdition; Who opposeth and exalteth himself above all that is called God, or that is worshipped; so that he as God sitteth in the temple of God, shewing himself that he is God. Remember ye not, that,

> *when I was yet with you, I told you these things? And now ye know what withholdeth that he might be revealed in his time. For the mystery of iniquity doth already work: only he who now letteth will let, until he be taken out of the way."*
> 2 Thessalonians 2:3–7

The Greek word used by the Apostle Paul for "mystery" is *mysterion*. According to *A Greek-English Lexicon of the New Testament and Other Early Christian Literature*, 3rd ed., (BDAG) this Greek word means "secret, transcendent, hidden reality."

In other words, the source of iniquity was being concealed from the general population. We see the symptoms within humanity as the rejection of the teachings of God regarding sin and the need for holiness. This fact of both the rejection of God's commandments and the rising sin within humanity is discovered in the Greek word used here by the apostle Paul for "iniquity," which is *anomia*. BDAG defines *anomia as* "a lawless frame of mind, those that despise the law."

Nimrod tapped deeply into the knowledge from the *nachash*. In Hebrew, the word for "serpent" is *nachash* which according to *Strong's Lexicon* means, "snake, serpent, fleeing serpent, or image of a serpent." However, in the *Companion Bible*, E.W. Bullinger reveals that the term also means "a shining one."

In *The Unseen Realm: Recovering the Supernatural Worldview of the Bible*, Dr. Michael Heiser brings even more clarity to the use of this ancient Hebrew word:

> *The Genesis "serpent" wasn't really a member of the animal kingdom. We have other passages to help us grasp that point, particularly in the New Testament. We understand that, even though New Testament writers refer to the serpent back in Eden, they are really referring to a supernatural entity—not a mere member of the animal kingdom.*

In Mark A. Flynn's book, *Forbidden Secrets of the Labyrinth: The*

Awakened Ones, the Hidden Destiny of America, and the Day after Tomorrow, he shares some of the historical etymology of this word:

> *Old English seraphim (plural), from Late Latin seraphim, from Greek seraphim, from Hebrew seraphim (only in Isaiah 6:2), plural of saraph probably literally "the burning one," from saraph "it burned." Seraphs were traditionally regarded as burning or flaming angels, though the word seems to have some etymological sense of "flying," perhaps from confusion with the root of Arabic sharafa, "be lofty." Some scholars identify it with a word found in other passages interpreted as "fiery flying serpent."*

There is nothing from Genesis 3 in which we can exegete that this serpent/*seraph* was Lucifer himself, although many theologians attribute this to Lucifer. This connection of the *seraph* of Genesis 3 with the cherub of Ezekiel 28 is due in part to these references in the book of Revelation:

> *And the great dragon was cast out, that old serpent, called the Devil, and Satan, which deceiveth the whole world: he was cast out into the earth, and his angels were cast out with him. Revelation 12:9*

Usually, we are taught that cherubim and seraphim are two separate classes of angels or immortals.

Nimrod's altered DNA may have given him access to the knowledge of the Watchers, dark wisdom which may very well be the origin of the gnostic concept of achieving godhood through the gaining of lost or hidden knowledge. It is a real possibility that Nimrod gained much more than simply a physical upgrade with his "transformation."

How did the knowledge of the Watchers survive the Flood and make it into the hands of Nimrod?

Researchers like Steve Quayle have documented how governments and secret societies are active in archeological digs today to discover information and technology from the Antediluvian Age. Therefore, it is not a stretch of the imagination to believe that Nimrod gained the knowledge and/or technology from the writings of the Watchers to empower his transformation into a giant.

CERN

In an earlier chapter I introduced Éliphas Lévi's Baphomet, the symbol of the goat pentagram. It is here I would like to interject an interesting point. Both Nimrod and the Baphomet are depicted as the Horned God Cernunnos, or Cern, an important deity in occultism. Interestingly enough, the word *Cern* can be found in ancient mythology. In Celtic mythology, the god *Cern* is depicted as having horns, recognized as the god of nature or fertility. Because of the association with various creatures, Cernunnos is sometimes described by scholars as "lord of the wild beasts."

We can see how Nimrod could be identified with Cern as the god of this world. In fact, Satan himself could be identified with Cern according to 2 Corinthians 4:4:

> *In whom the god of this world hath blinded the minds of them which believe not, lest the light of the glorious gospel of Christ, who is the image of God, should shine unto them.*

I find it interesting, especially when it comes to technology, that CERN, based in Switzerland, is the acronym for the French *Conseil Européen pour la Recherche Nucléaire* (or, in English, the European Organization for Nuclear Research). It is a provisional body founded in 1952 with the mandate to establish a world-class fundamental physics research organization. Activated in 2008, CERN is gearing up for another run at smashing particles together to unlock the secrets of the universe. It boasts the largest particle physics laboratory in the world. CERN has approved plans to build a $23 billion super-collider 100 km in circumference (62 miles) that would make the current 27 km 16 teraelectron volt (TeV) Large Hadron Collider (LHC) look tiny in comparison.

I myself have outlined on many shows the occult connections with CERN. Since its unveiling in 2004, CERN's statue of the dancing Shiva, the destroyer god, in the Nataraja dance, causes many to question the true motives of CERN.

Shiva is one of the main deities of Hinduism. He is part of the *Trimurti*, the Hindu trinity.

The Nataraja depiction shows Shiva as the cosmic dancer who performs a divine dance to destroy a weary universe. The statue shows Shiva in the middle of a circle of flames with his left leg raised and balancing over the demonic dwarf Apasmara who represents ignorance. Apasmara, in Hindu mythology, is a demon that cannot be killed so Shiva uses his right foot to crush and subdue him during the Nataraja dance.

The statue of Shiva at CERN contains an inscription of a quote by physicist Fritjof Capra, which states: "Hundreds of years ago, Indian artists created visual images of dancing Shivas in a beautiful series of bronzes. In our time, physicists have used the most advanced technology to portray the patterns of the cosmic dance. The metaphor of the cosmic dance thus unifies ancient mythology and modern physics."

More recently, Capra explained that:

> "Modern physics has shown that the rhythm of creation and destruction is not only manifest in the turn of the seasons and in the birth and death of all living creatures, but is also the very essence of inorganic matter," and that "for the modern physicists, then, Shiva's dance is the dance of subatomic matter."

Given the mythology behind the statue and the type of scientific pioneering CERN represents, plus the circle of flame representing a stargate-like portal, we have Shiva representing Satan traveling though the portal to destroy the church, subdue God, and take over the world. There are those who believe CERN and the LHC will be instrumental in this process. CERN's official logo resembles three sixes, the biblical Mark of The Beast from the book of Revelation.

This also resembles a hand gesture that is thought to signify the three sixes of the Mark of The Beast. But most people, outside of those of us who question, often deduce CERN's logo represents nothing else but the design of synchrotron particle accelerators.

Way back in 2009, Sergio Bertolucci, Director for Research and Scientific Computing at CERN told reporters, "Out of this door might come something, or we might send something through it."[3]

Then, in 2015, General Rolf Heuer, general director of CERN, says CERN will "open the door" from our physical universe to non-physical universes, which will allow human scientists to interact face-to-face with non-physical beings.

And Bertolucci said CERN will act as a type of portal, to allow these non-Earth entities to come into our physical world and be with us.[4]

I leave it to you to decide whether we have a massive coincidence or a massive conspiracy at CERN connected to the second coming of fallen gods, but I believe personally it is very plausible that CERN will have something to do with opening either the spiritual veil or the bottomless pit described in Revelation 9.

Speaking of portals and gates, could Nimrod's tower represent some kind of techno-portal, or gate, inspired by the forbidden secret technology of the fallen?

---

3. https://www.theregister.com/2009/11/06/lhc_dimensional_portals/

4. https://www.thedailyreporter.com/article/20150901/NEWS/150909972

It is fascinating that Babel has been a powerful symbol in the history of technology, telepathy and cybernetics.

> "Come, let us build ourselves a city, and a tower whose top is in the heavens." Genesis 11:4

Incredibly ironic is a 1961 edition of Communications of the ACM (Association for Computer Machinery) using the image of the Tower of Babel on its cover. That edition, a collection of papers given at the ACM Compiler Symposium from the year before, shows a ziggurat tower extending into the clouds, covered with computing terms and acronyms. The base of the tower reads, "Babel 1960." The June 17, 1971 edition of New Scientist and Science Journal likewise referenced the Tower of Babel regarding computer language development. Then, in an IBM press release on March 20, 2008, the headline read, *"IBM, Forterra Using Unified Communications in Virtual Worlds to Solve 'Tower of Babel' for Intelligence Agencies,"* announcing a virtual reality sharing system. The article outlines a futuristic unified communications solution code named "Babel Bridge" that could allow U.S. intelligence agencies to instantly communicate within a virtual world.

And when IBM introduced its Internet of Things Foundation – "internet of things" (IoT) is the networking of connected devices – John R. Thompson, Vice President of the IBM IoT Foundation, described IoT this way: *"At the end of the day, it's the Tower of Babel."*[5]

Babel is synonymous with idolatry. Drawing on ancient texts, Professor Yehezkel Kaufmann described the Babel experience this way:

> "Man's rebellion reached its peak. He wished to storm heaven, to be 'like God,' to rule the world."[6]

Where have we heard that before?

---

5. Thomas Claburn, "IBM Lays Internet of Things Foundation," online edition, April 28, 2015.
6. Yehezkel Kaufmann, The Religion of Israel: From Its Beginnings to the Babylonian Exile.
(The University of Chicago Press, 1960, translated and abridged by Moshe Greenberg), p.294.

Sometime during the building phase, God comes down to examine the construction. As Man builds to assert his unifying ascension, God intervenes. To man's desire to make a name for himself, God responds. God – who cannot share His glory, ultimately and rightly brings judgment. Babel is history's reminder of idolatry and judgment – that God Himself will step-in when Man ultimately oversteps.[7]

The tantalizing illusion of technology and advancement paving the way for godhood possibilities is the penultimate human hubris. (And remember, Lucifer fell due to his pride. We must discern good and evil so we do not follow suit.)

The spurious antediluvian mysticism honoring the Dark Angels, marked by initiations reserved for only the Elite, complete with secret ceremonies and abominable rituals, led the naive people of Day 6 into corruption, violence, and greed, which culminated with the creation of Nephilim. The incredible knowledge and technology encouraged by Fallen Angels led to building great cities and spectacular monuments, as well as the unbridled use of gene manipulation.

That same Fallen Angel Technology and knowledge now dominates our culture and is connected to the illicit heavenly knowledge that caused the Flood catastrophe, and the rebellion at Babel.

There is a real possibility that when God created the angels He encoded within their spiritual DNA all of the information they needed to serve Him. Adam may have been created the same way (in a limited sense). In the temptation of Adam and Eve by the *nachash*, this *seraph* was promising them "knowledge," accusing God of holding out on them or withholding information from them. In truth, when Adam and Eve fell, they were cut off from the knowledge of God, because they had accepted knowledge from another source.

---
7. Carl Teichrib, Games of Gods, 2018.

What if the Watchers' spiritual DNA passed on their knowledge to their children the same way we pass on information to our children and grandchildren? We do see a hint of this referenced by the apostle Paul when he referred to Believers as "casting off mortality for immortality and the corruptible for incorruptible." 1 Corinthians 15:52 In our new glorified state, we will be completely connected back to Almighty God and will draw from His knowledge to serve Him perfectly for all eternity.

It could be said that Nimrod discovered some ancient technology of the Watchers that corrupted his DNA to the place where he became a *gibbor* or "giant." His new altered state of being opened his mind to the knowledge of the Watchers, and he became proficient in the use of the Dark Force.

When God saw what they intended to do at the Tower of Babel, it is also possible that He not only divided the people, but also the knowledge that they had been given as well. From my personal research into the Mystery Religions, it seems that they have been laboring since the Tower of Babel to reconstruct this lost knowledge.

The builder of the world's first one-world government, with its capital at the Tower of Babel, was Nimrod, who was a Nephilim. When you view this in the context of Science - or Alchemy - or better yet, techno-sorcery, we see that Nimrod chose to allow himself to be fully embraced by the dark forces. Could building the tower be an attempt by Fallen Angels to get humans to co-operate with them in constructing their former abode, thus — finishing their attempt at overthrowing God from His throne?

At Babel, a new strategy was to create a means to rise up and assault the gates of Heaven. This required time and technology. The fallen ones could not return to Heaven on their own; they were banished. In order to make their assault, they needed the willing participation of humans.

Note that God took notice of this building project, and decided to confuse the languages of men and tear down the tower.

> *"If we do not do this, then nothing will be kept from them, that they conceive."* Genesis 11:6

Think about how unusual a statement is. God is God. He can do whatever He wants, but the building of this tower was of concern to Him? *"Nothing will be kept from them."* How odd…

The tower represented something unique, a willing participation between Fallen Angels and humans. The satanic plan was to somehow unite willing humans with Fallen Angels, in an attempt to return 'home.'

Towers, monoliths, pyramids, mountains and all places of dark worship, stood as reminders to humans that they were being directed to look upwards, to the heavens.

Patiently, these dark forces waited, *suggesting* to men new technologies and innovations, the discovery of new materials and concepts that would eventually lead to today's "information and technology revolution" — which is nothing more than a return to the knowledge known at the time of the Tower of Babel.

When Francis Bacon planned for America to be head of the New World Order and the "New Atlantis," he was aware of these themes. The New World Order will be headed by the Antichrist, and the "New Atlantis," according to Plato, is the model of a society ruled by a technocratic Elite with a genetic heritage going back to Mount Hermon (where the Watchers made their pact to break God's rule of "everything after its own kind" and mate with human women). Just as the hybrid species of Fallen Angels and human women produced a soulless race, that soulless race possessed advanced technologies and initiated the satanic and pagan worship of Baal, Ashtoreth, and other gods that dominated the land of Canaan under the Nephilim giants.

Soulless beings, by their very programming, automatically come under the rule of Lucifer, because Lucifer, his Fallen Angels, and mankind who choose to serve him are either soulless, or the Holy Spirit is deactivated in those who consciously reject God's free offer of salvation in Christ.

Satan is the god of this world and seeks to remake it "in his image." He can't be omnipresent like God, but perhaps with the right technology…

The book of Enoch provides an account of how the Watchers came and began teaching men forbidden knowledge.

> "Thou seest what Azâzêl hath done, who hath taught all unrighteousness on earth and revealed the eternal secrets which were (preserved) in heaven, which men were striving to learn." 1 Enoch 9:6

The statement, "which men were striving to learn," summarizes the very foundation of all esoteric societies. Their main focus is discovering and implementing the forbidden knowledge brought to humanity by the "old gods." Members of these societies, in conjunction with nefarious clandestine think tanks and top-secret agencies such as DARPA, want to rediscover this lost Fallen Angel technology.

When we examine the writings of the prophets of the Old Testament and the book of Revelation, we discover a startling truth regarding the last days: We will be facing a combination of the Genesis 6 Watcher invasion and the time of Nimrod and the Tower of Babel! No wonder Jesus declared:

> For then shall be great tribulation, such as was not since the beginning of the world to this time, no, nor ever shall be. And except those days should be shortened, there should no flesh be saved: but for the elect's sake those days shall be shortened. Matthew 24:21–22

Mankind has come to the point in history where he is, technologically, able to do most anything that he conceives. With many of these technological and scientific breakthroughs "guided" directly or indirectly by Satan, we stand at a precipice in time when the greater "master plan" of dark forces can be realized and acted upon.

CHAPTER 8
ALIEN-TECH: THE NAZIS, UFOS & THE OCCULT CONNECTION

"Any sufficiently advanced technology is indistinguishable from magic." ~ Arthur C. Clarke

The things that once were fodder for science-fiction discussions are now on the cover of Modern Science. And on the silver screen...

Fifty years ago, comic books were full of propaganda for the Fallen. The gods themselves were redrawn as characters for the comics, especially Thor and the Norse pantheon, although just about every one of the gods of the ancient world has appeared in Marvel or DC Comics at some point. Other superheroes are thinly-veiled analogues for ancient deities. These gods in Spandex are based on entities that God has judged and condemned to death—*because they want to destroy the human race.*

Marvel Comics contains many elements of the themes outlined in this book. Marvel's infamous "Captain America" and spin-offs check off the boxes of all the dark elements: Genetic Tampering, Nazi Eugenics, Deep Lab Experiments, CIA MkUltra Mind-Control,

Bio-Tech Enhancement, DNA Augmenting, Super Soldiers, Robotic Prosthetics and yes, Alien Technology.

In the comic, Captain Steven "Steve" Rogers, upon America's entry into World War II, was rejected from serving in the United States Army despite several attempts to enlist. Rogers ultimately volunteered for *Project Rebirth* (interesting name) where he was the recipient of Super Soldier Serum developed and perfected by Abraham Erskine under the Strategic Scientific Reserve (SSR). As a result, the SSR started Project Rebirth, the augmenting initiative to turn Allied soldiers into super soldiers. The scientific elixir greatly augmented Rogers' physical abilities to superhuman levels. One could say he became a Superman, *Übermensch*.

In the comic, Project Rebirth, also called Operation: Rebirth, Weapons Plus, the Bio-Tech Force Enhancement Program and the Super Soldier Program, were all United States government projects initiated in the 1940s during World War II, with the goal to transform Allied soldiers into super soldiers. Eventually the serum was destroyed and the only hope to recreate Erskine's formula was locked in Rogers' genetic code. In other words, the "secretive super soldier serum" remained in Rogers' DNA.

Sound familiar?

In May of 2021, Marvel's *The Falcon and the Winter Soldier* brought us details about Captain America's lifelong friend, Bucky Barnes *aka The Winter Soldier*. While Bucky Barnes didn't receive the super-serum that his friend Captain America did, he did endure repeated MK ultra-type brainwashing, rituals and experiments where he was programmed as an elite assassin for high-level black ops, or as I call it, *killer programming*. Winter Soldier is essentially a brain-washed killing machine with an augmented prosthetic made out of *Wakandan* technology. *Wakanda*, the home of *Black Panther*, is a reclusive kingdom in Africa with extraordinarily powerful alien technology.

Notice that, *Alien Tech…*

Back to real life… In the summer of 1945, John F. Kennedy was a guest of Navy Secretary James Forrestal in a post-war tour of Germany. Kennedy personally witnessed technological secrets that have to-date not been disclosed to the general public. These secrets stemmed from technologies that Nazi Germany had acquired from around the world, and were attempting to develop for their weapons programs.

These advanced technologies stunned the military government running the U.S. zone of occupied Germany. How did the Nazis develop them? The answer, according to the father of German rocket design, Herman Oberth, was just as stunning. He said, *"We cannot take all the credit for our record advancements in certain scientific fields alone; we have been helped by the people of other worlds."*[1]

Some "Ancient Astronaut Theorists" suggest the *Ahnenerbe* – an elite Nazi institute – had discovered extraterrestrial technology, and that Germany used it to create their highly advanced military weapons and other high-tech during and well beyond WWII.

At any rate, these Nazi technologies were definitely "out of this world" in origin.

The Vril Society

The Vril Society was a group of high-level practitioners of the dark arts, that "channeled communications to alien races." It sought to form a Utopian New World order led by alternative science and technology, with the use of the swastika to represent high-level occultism. They advanced the idea of a subterranean matriarchal utopia ruled by a race of Aryan beings who had mastered a mysterious

1. https://www.azquotes.com/quote/615728

force called Vril. The Vril Society was led by Maria Orsic, a noted Austrian medium. Orsic endorsed the German national movement to annex Austria with the German Reich. In 1919, Orsic met with members of the *Thule Society* in a hunting lodge near Berchtesgaden, Germany. The purpose of the meeting was to lay out the telepathic messages she had been given. According to her Vrillian sidekick, Sigrun, the messages came from Aldebaran (in the constellation of Taurus) located about 68 light years from Earth.

Orsic, in a trance, scribbled strange symbols on a piece of paper. One series of messages was written in a language that Orsic did not recognize but thought to be German Templar script. The second set of messages was completely unrecognizable. With the help of Thule society members, the scripts were examined and deemed to be legitimate ancient Sumerian texts, a dead language used in Babylonian times. The writing disclosed that the Sumi, a humanoid race, had colonized the Earth 500 million years ago and were known as the *Atlantians*. The Sumi explained that they were ancestors of the modern-day Aryan race. Translators determined they were actually messages that contained instructions for building a flying machine that operated off of a mysterious energy source.

Interesting to note that mention of these flying machines was made nearly 1,000 years earlier in the poem, *Samarangana Sutradhara*. It describes construction of flying machines that sound eerily similar to the Vril aircraft:

> *"Strong and durable must the body of the Vimana be made, like a great flying bird of light material. Inside one must put the mercury engine with its iron heating apparatus underneath. By means of the power latent in the mercury, which sets the driving whirlwind in motion, a man sitting inside may travel a great distance in the sky. The movements of a Vimana are such that it can vertically ascend, vertically descend, or move slanting forwards and backwards. With*

the help of machines, human beings can fly through the air and heavenly beings can come down to Earth."

The Vril Society was one of the major occult societies that helped fuel Nazism in Germany. In the book, *The Black Sun*, author Peter Moon provides some basic information on its formation and its beliefs:

The Vril Society began around the same time as the Thule Society when Karl Haushofer founded the "Brüder des Lichts," which means "Brothers of the Light." This is sometimes referred to as the Luminous Lodge. This group was eventually renamed the Vril-Gesellschaft as it rose in prominence and united three major secret societies: the Lords of the Black Stone, having emerged from the Teutonic Order in 1917; the Black Knights of the Thule Society; and the Black Sun, later identified as the elite of Heinrich Himmler's SS.

The Vril Flying Machine

The flying machine construction plans that Orsic and Sigrun "received from the Aldebaran planet," were rushed to the *University of Munich* where they were examined in detail by Dr. W. O. Schumann who concluded that they did indeed contain extremely advanced engineering specifications and the decision was made to attempt to build the strange energy-powered craft.

By 1922, parts for the flying machine began arriving from various industrial sources, with financing provided by the occultic Thule Society, of which Hitler was a devout member.

The plans detailed a machine whose principle of flight utilized circular discs spun in counter rotation, reminiscent of the Old Testament's "fiery chariot" mentioned in the book of Ezekiel that spun *like a wheel within a wheel.*

During the Construction efforts in 1923, Hitler rose to power

TECHNOGEDDON

and the *National Socialist Party* began working even closer with Vril, since they held the same Utopian New World ideologies.

The Vril Spaceship finally reached conclusion in 1934.

The *RFZ-2*, as it was dubbed, was successfully test-flown. Nazi interest in the unusual aircraft peaked and the Black Sun, the magi division of the *Nazi SS*, took over the project. Development continued at a slow pace while other groups competed for funds with Nazi Luftwaffe war planes.

In 1941, another craft, the *Vril-2*, was put into production. The Nazi craft employed the Schumann-Levitator drive for vertical lift. The *Vril-2* production crew noted that the engine produced unusually dramatic effects when accelerated. Descriptions of blurred contours and emissions of luminous ionization colors were included in their research reports.

On January 22, 1944, a meeting was held with Hitler, Himmler, Dr. Schumann, and Kunkel of Vril, to discuss the 68 light-year "trip" to a galaxy far, far away...

The Vril Society believed this "channeled energy" could be transformed into a viable technological reality.

Speaking of the occult and channeling, throughout Aleister Crowley's years as a magus, and his many magical experiments, he often attempted to contact *entities*. Through the uttering of incantations and the regurgitation of ancient inscriptions and veiled verses, Crowley called forward all manner of spirits, demons and invisible masters from which he sought counsel. One particular entity, or, at least, icon of the Crowleian pantheon that draws an intense amount of interest, is the character known as 'LAM'. Around 1917, in New York, after performing a ritual now known as the "Alamantrah Working," Crowley channeled and then drew the image of this *praeter-human intelligence*.

What's interesting about Crowley's drawing of LAM is the stark resemblance it bears to the popular image of the "Alien Greys" of today, when in fact Crowley drew his image 2 decades before the UFO boom which followed the Roswell incident in the 40s.

Time-Tech

Perhaps one of the intriguing elements of the uranium oxide mines in Poland's Beskidy Mountains and the direct SS presence around them may be connected to the "secret weapon" of the Nazis, *Die Glocke*, or "The Nazi Bell." This otherworld device, constructed by some of the finest scientific minds under the Third Reich, would first come to light in the 2000 book, *The Truth About the Wonder Weapon*, by Polish author and researcher, Igor Witkowski.

He claimed to have made the discovery from the leaked files of Nazi SS officer Jakob Sporrenberg (executed in 1952 for war crimes), files which were given to him by a contact in the Polish intelligence services.

The drive of the Nazi Bell was anti-gravity technology and propulsion. Inside the interior surface of the bell was a "mirror-like" material. According to the leaked files, when the device was active, this mirror-interior would fill with "visions of the past or future." It was alleged that the Bell had the ability to "bend time and space." If Witkowski's translations were true, the Nazis had a bona-fide time-machine.

The experiments and testing of the Nazi Bell, according to Witkowski, took place at a site nicknamed "The Henge" along the Czech and Polish border. The object itself was approximately 15-feet high and 9-feet across. The exterior contained mysterious Egyptian-like writing along its base.

Later, in the 1960s, Father Pellegrino Ernetti, an Italian physicist and Benedictine monk, helped create a time-machine, dubbed *The Chronovisor*. From the founding of the Roman Empire to the destruction of Sodom and Gomorrah, to the Romans crucifying Jesus Christ, Ernetti alleged that with the help of the device, he and his team had taken a peek into some of the most important events in history. On May 2, 1972, an Italian publication called *La Domenica del Corriere* published his claim. Titled "*A Machine That Photographs The Past Has Been Invented*," the article covered Ernetti's shocking statements for all of Italy to read. The article purported that *Ernetti* "*had witnessed the Last Supper and kept a photograph of the Biblical event for himself as a souvenir.*"

Ernetti claimed that he and a group of renowned scientists built the machine in a mutual quest to uncover the past. One scientist was Fermi, who won the Nobel Prize in Physics in 1938, and the other was none other than the infamous Wernher Von Braun, the German-born aerospace engineer and space architect whose work at NASA got America to the moon. Von Braun had been the leading figure in the development of rocket and space technology in Nazi Germany.

NASA does not name objects by coincidence. Its Horizon Mission target, an object about 4 billion miles from Earth, is called *Ultima Thule*.

Mark Showalter, a planetary astronomer and investigator who led the naming process, told *Newsweek*:

> "[It is] beyond the limits of the known world. People have applied the term to distant, cold, northern lands—both mythological ones and the real Arctic."[2]

And speaking of the Artic…

Operation High-Jump

"Operation High-Jump" was a U.S.-led multi-national effort to

---

2. *Newsweek*, NASA named Its Next New Horizon Ultimate Thule, A Mythical Land with a Nazi Connection, March 2018.

establish a permanent base at the South Pole. It turned out to be a "close encounter of the third kind."

In 1947, highly respected and decorated Air Force pilot Admiral Richard E. Byrd of the United States Navy, flew a reconnaissance flight 1,700 miles beyond the North Pole. He reported by radio that he saw below him, not ice and snow, but land areas consisting of mountains, forests, green vegetation, lakes and rivers, and he said he saw, in the underbrush, a strange animal resembling the mammoth found frozen in Arctic ice.[3] Evidently, he had entered a warmer region than the icebound Territory that extends from the Pole to Siberia.

His claims, which would make world news, were spine-chilling. He detailed a "huge opening" and then found himself "*inside the Earth*" (hollow-earth theory). He recounted entering a "strange abyss" when something took control of his aircraft. Suddenly, several strange saucer-shaped "flying crafts" surrounded his plane. Each craft bore a Nazi-style swastika and markings.

Several weeks later, he would speak at several press conferences with reporters from around the world. His statements appeared in several newspapers, including a March 5, 1947 story that ran in the *El Mercurio* newspaper in Santiago, Chile. In the article he said the continental United States would be "*attacked by flying objects that could fly from pole to pole at incredible speeds.*"

Ray Palmer, a leading American expert on flying saucers, is of the opinion that Admiral Byrd's discoveries in the Arctic and Antarctic regions offer an explanation of the origin of the flying saucers, which, he believes, do not come from other planets, but from the hollow interior of the earth, where exists an advanced civilization possessing highly advanced technology and aeronautics. Palmer notes:

---
3. http://www.deepinfo2.com/Byrd.htm

> "They are the creators of the flying saucers, which are operated by this superior power, drawn from the electromagnetism of the atmosphere. Also, the gigantic size of the human beings dwelling in the Earth's interior corresponds to the great size of its animal life, as observed by Admiral Byrd, who, during his flight beyond the North Pole, observed a strange creature resembling an ancient mammoth."

The book, *The Smoky God*, written in 1908 by Willis George Emerson, describes a Norse father and son's experience when their small fishing boat encountered an extraordinary windstorm which carried them through a polar opening into a "hollow Earth." They spent two years there and returned through the south polar opening. The father lost his life when an iceberg broke in two and destroyed the boat. The son was rescued and subsequently spent 24 years in prison for insanity, as a result of detailing his experience. When he was in his nineties, he told his story to Emerson. He relinquished the maps that he had made of the interior of the Earth, and the manuscripts describing his experiences. The book chronicles the "people" who dwell inside the Earth, whom he and his father met during their visit, and whose language they learned. He said that they lived to 800 years and were in possession of highly advanced science and technology. They could telepathically transmit their thoughts from one to another by certain sources of power greater than the electricity of today.

The conspiracies surrounding Antarctic and the Nazi presence around the South Pole are interesting enough.

Are these sightings a continuation of alien-Nazi occult technology?

And what of the Vril Society, which became the inner circle of the Thule Society Sorcerers, whose focus was on establishing communications with ancient *god-men*?

It is vital to know that much of the work done in Germany by Nazi scientists, including Von Braun, continued in America under *Operation Paperclip*.

Operation Paperclip was a secret program of the Joint Intelligence Objectives Agency (JIOA) in which more than 1,600 German scientists, engineers, and technicians (such as Von Braun and his V-2 rocket team) were brought from Germany to the United States for government employment, primarily between 1945 and 1959. Many were members and former leaders of the Nazi Party. In her book, *Secret Technologies Invented by the Nazis*, Annie Jacobsen exposes a treacherous time at the end of World War II when our government was "secretly colluding with the now-defunct German Reich to bring Nazi Scientists home to America, to leadership of NASA, to high-ranking positions in the American Academy including – Rocket Science, Physics, Chemistry, Aeronautics, Electronics (guidance systems, radar, satellites), Architecture, Medicine, Science, Engineering and Weapons Technology."[4]

With the blood of thousands on his hands, SS General Hans Kammler killed himself in 1945 in the dying days of Hitler's Germany. The man steeped in the horrors of the Nazi death camps had met his fate. That, at least, was the official story.

It is now claimed that Kammler survived the war and was spirited away to America and given a new identity by the US authorities.[5]

In his book, *The SS Brotherhood of the Bell: The Nazis' Incredible Secret Technology*, historian Joseph P. Farrell details that the United States, Germany, and Japan were in an arms-race for something they knew was possible: the atomic bomb. For esoteric societies within these nations, the atomic bomb was the weapon of the gods.

---

4. *Secret Technologies Invented by the Nazis*, Annie Jacobsen, Operation Paperclip: The Secret Intelligence Program That Brought Nazi Scientists to America (New York: Back Bay Books, 2014).
5. https://www.dailymail.co.uk/news/article-2653919/Did-Americans-fake-Nazis-WWII-suicide-spirit-away-US-hands-Hitlers-secret-weapons-programme.html

In the book, *Occult Secrets of VRIL*, anthropologist Robert Sepehr suggests that Robert Oppenheimer was not the originator of the atomic bomb, but only rediscovered this ancient "weapon of the gods."

Oppenheimer's reference to atomic weapons being used in prehistory seems to confirm this esoteric belief. Although a nuclear weapon is certainly the most destructive of the supposed ancient technologies of the gods, it is not the only technology nations seek.

In his documentary, *True Legends: Technology of the Fallen*, Steve Quayle notes that both secret societies and intelligence agencies from around the globe are actively seeking advanced ancient technologies in archeological sites around the world. They continue the task started by Hitler and the Nazis: to discover the technology of the Aryans and reverse-engineer it.

When peering through the lens of the history of Nazis, it is easy to see they were heavily influenced by the Watchers and their sophisticated *superpowers*.

CHAPTER 9

COVID, DNA & THE GOD CODE

"When you're born again, your DNA changes. You have the ability to understand God's terms." ~ Bill McCartney

As shown in previous chapters, Transhumanists reject the biblical account of Creation that says God created man in His own image. Originally, in the Garden of Eden, Adam and Eve had the completely pure and uncorrupted DNA of God. They disobeyed God's only commandment and released the death force—activating the law of sin and death into all of creation.

Do not be deceived: God cannot be mocked.

The Word states that the Last Days hold extreme deception for most of humanity and many will show loyalty to the Man of Sin—the Antichrist who appears on the scene working lying signs, wonders and miracles.

What kind of lie will be *so* convincing that it leads an enormous amount of the world's population to eternal separation from God as warned about in the book of Revelation?

It's the kind that starts slowly, as a promise of a bright future in science and technology, vowing that the future generations will be smarter, more efficient, healthier, and live longer.

It involves "improving the human condition;" it involves *playing God* and making gods.

The law of God is written on mankind's hearts, or inner being. It's God's special programming that runs the software of God, which is the body, soul, and spirit. Let's call it the *God Code*.

Even our DNA contains the God Code.

But what if Satan, in an effort to snuff out the very God Code within mankind, was able to pull off the biggest mass human genome experiment ever? A maniacal way to make humans accept the unthinkable, and literally erase the very God Code within us?

Enter Craig Venter. In 2010, Craig Venter (one of those involved in mapping the human genome), made history by creating what he dubbed "synthetic life" (which was actually a living cell into which he inserted additional genetic material). How does a guy who swims out to the middle of the ocean to commit suicide come back to shore and become a genius with "knowledge" for the human genome project? Remember that name, Craig Venter.

He wants to patent humans and turn them into the property of pharmaceutical companies through injections which contain exotic nanobots and other futuristic tech. The human genome stretches out 10 million miles and it is the blueprint of God and Venter wants to be God. Does he want to write out the God Code and insert his own? Hold that thought.

And now . . . the COVID Vaccine

In 2013, a mysterious new flu virus hit the world. It was the H7N9 strain of bird flu, and by the time it infected 120 and killed 23, researchers still didn't know how it was transmitted or how to stop it. As the virus arrived in the dense Chinese province of Hunan, health officials began to fear the worst. They called Dan Gibson.

Gibson was Vice President of DNA Technology at Synthetic Genomics, the research institute founded in 2005 by, guess who? Craig Venter.

Among its research milestones, the institute created the first synthetic cell, designed in a computer and DNA-printed completely from scratch. Dan Gibson, Venter's hireling, was given a download link to the DNA sequence of the bird flu virus and told to do one thing: design a vaccine.

On December 31, 2019, Chinese authorities in Wuhan announced a cluster of pneumonia cases of unknown etiology, which included patients who reported exposure to Wuhan's Huanan Seafood wholesale market. On January 9, 2020, the Chinese Center for Disease Control reported that a novel coronavirus was the causative agent. Shortly thereafter the genomic sequences of several isolates became publicly available.

On February 10, 2020, the WHO named the disease caused by the new coronavirus COVID-19, and the new virus was named severe acute respiratory syndrome coronavirus 2 (SARS-CoV-2). Genomic analyses indicated that SARS-CoV-2 shared genomic similarities with SARS-CoV within the receptor-binding motif that directly contacts the human receptor ACE2. This had major implications for vaccine design and as such The World Health Organization (WHO) declared COVID-19 a global pandemic.

There are very unsavory characters in the "plandemic" agenda including, not surprisingly, Ray Kurzweil, Anthony Fauci, Bill Gates, Klaus Schwab (WEF), and many others. But the man who really appears to be the head of the snake is Craig Venter, the man who mapped DNA.

Gene therapy was touted back in 2015, when a New York Times article reported, "Developing vaccine technology called immunoprophylaxis by gene transfer." As the Times reported, animal tests on the synthetic DNA vaccine:

> *"Are essentially re-engineering the animals to resist disease."*

It went on to say:

> *"…the prospect of genetically engineering people to resist infectious diseases may raise concerns among patients."*

Now, in the aftermath of the COVID pandemic, human beings are set to be genetically altered with mRNA vaccine technology based on synthetic biology. Synthetic biologists, many funded by Bill Gates, believe that they can "do better" than nature with "self-assembling nanoparticles" that will be injected into your body.[1]

> *"With all due respect to nature, synthetic biologists believe they can do better. Using computers, they are designing new, self-assembling protein nanoparticles studded with viral proteins, called antigens: these porcupine-like particles would be the guts of a vaccine."*[2]

Others do not hide their arrogance at all:

Tom Knight, formerly a senior research scientist at the MIT Computer Science and Artificial Intelligence Laboratory says:

> *"The genetic code is 3.6 billion years old. It's time for a rewrite."*

Now, Knight's synthetic biology company Ginkgo Bioworks is using its synthetic biology tech to develop COVID vaccines, too.

As I wrote in my book Green Gospel,

> *"In 1994, two critics of the UN's Agenda 21 wrote, 'the main stake raised by the biodiversity convention is the issue of ownership and control over biological diversity… the major concern was protecting the pharmaceutical and emerging biotechnology industries, including immunizations through technological advancements.'"*[3]

---

1. https://www.statnews.com/2020/03/09/coronavirus-scientists-play-legos-with-proteins-to-build-next-gen-vaccine/
2. Ibid.
3. https://www.amazon.com/Green-Gospel-New-World-Religion/dp/1632325225

Nothing more clear than that!

Let's go back to Dr. Craig Venter, who as I said earlier was credited with creating "synthetic life." As revealed in the 2005 book, *The Google Story*, Google founders Larry Page and Sergey Brin met with Craig Venter at the Edge Billionaires meeting: a secretive gathering in LA. The Edge Billionaire dinner – comparable to the secretive Bilderberg group – is an annual gathering of tech elites that has hosted Page, Epstein, Gates, Venter, Jeff Bezos, Bill Joy and many others.

The Edge billionaire meetings discuss the future of genetic engineering, biocomputation and re-designing humanity in a Transhumanist era…

Physicist Freeman Dyson described the individuals leading this group as having god-like power to create entirely new species on earth in a "New Age of Wonder." As he describes them:

> "…a new generation of artists, writing genomes as fluently as Blake and Byron wrote verses, might create an abundance of new flowers and fruit and trees and birds to enrich the ecology of our planet."[4]

Satanic Billionaire Megalomaniacs Patenting life. Nothing scary here…

It appeared Venter needed help to unlock the molecular mysteries of life and it seems he may have thought that Google's mathematicians, scientists, technologists, and computing power had the potential to vault his research forward. After all, Google had already downloaded a map of the human genome and its founders were quietly working on molecular biology and genetics.

Just think about that, the guy (Venter) who wants to patent humans and turn them into the property of pharmaceutical companies by injecting them with nanobots and genome altering

---

4. https://www.edge.org/3rd_culture/age_of_wonder10/age_of_wonder_index.html

TECHNOGEDDON

tech, teaming up with the world's most tremendous database and immense computing power in the world.

Mad scientists converging on millions of genes in combination with massive amounts of biological and scientific data.

Talk about a match made in hell...

Now evil "Mr. Computer-virus" Gates, who has poured boatloads of cash into vaccines, has taken a page from Venter and Google, using synthetic biology and genetic code created by computers, in the coronavirus vaccine. Gates and his paid lemmings believe they can "do better" than nature with self-assembling nanoparticles that will be injected into your body.

As reported by CBS in 2017, The Gates Foundation gave Moderna Therapeutics $100 million to develop mRNA-based vaccines for infectious diseases.

Another Gates-funded Malaria vaccine technology from Inovio aims to use electrical current to open cells and deliver synthetic DNA. But the Gates Foundation hasn't just handed over money to drug makers; it's also invested in a few of them. Some of the coronavirus vaccine stocks that the Gates Foundation is betting on are: Pfizer, BioNTech, CureVac and Vir Biotechnology, partnered with GlaxoSmithKline.[5]

Talk about Pharmakia, aka sorcery! These modern-day sorcerers are peddling their slick "demon tech" under the glossy veneer of "keeping you safe" while *merchandizing the souls of men.* Revelation 18:12-14

The modern term "pharmacology" (where we get pharmacist, pharmacy, etc.) emerged from *pharmakeia.*

Strong's Concordance-*pharmakeia*: the use of medicine, drugs or spells. Original Word: sorcery or witchcraft. One variation means a *"spell-giving potion"* by a witch or magician.

---
5. https://www.msn.com/en-us/money/companies/4-coronavirus-vaccine-stocks-the-bill-melinda-gates-foundation-is-betting-on/ar-BB19nssN

It is interesting that Revelation 18:23 reads,

"And the light of a candle shall shine no more at all in thee; and the voice of the bridegroom and of the bride shall be heard no more at all in thee: for thy merchants were the great men of the earth; for by thy sorceries were all nations deceived."

Did you catch that? *"By thy sorceries were all nations deceived."*

Bill Gates, the sorcery king himself, also invests in Dr. Fauci's *National Institute of Allergy and Infectious Diseases (NIAID)* program *Global Vaccine Action Plan*. Reportedly, Dr. Fauci owns a patent for a specific type of COVID vaccine and stands to collect half of the royalties from Pfizer, Merck, GlaxoSmithKline, and Sanofi. The companies that used the patents have to split the profits with the NIAID and the Gates Foundation.[6]

Many of the COVID-19 vaccines currently being fast-tracked are not conventional vaccines. Their design is aimed at manipulating your very biology, and therefore they have the potential to alter the biology of the entire human race. The mRNA COVID-19 vaccine will be the first of its kind.

Conventional vaccines train your body to recognize and respond to the proteins of a particular virus by injecting a small amount of the actual viral protein into your body, thereby triggering an immune response and the development of antibodies. This is not what happens with an mRNA vaccine. In this vaccine they use something called "transfection." A technology used in GMO *franken-food* production such as what Monsanto uses.

This is the first time in history it would be used on humans.

Moderna Inc, one of the COVID vaccine front-runners, is an American pharmaceutical and biotechnology company based in Cambridge, Massachusetts, that partners with Takeda Pharmaceutical

---

6. https://www.irishcentral.com/news/robert-f-kennedy-jr-dr-fauci-covid19-vaccine

TECHNOGEDDON

Company in Japan. Moderna is heavily funded by the Bill and Melinda Gates Foundation and was given $100 billion by the US government and issued emergency use authorization to manufacture COVID mRNA vaccines.

Prior to COVID, Moderna had never developed a vaccine or even a human medicine, for that matter. Ever.

Moderna went from being an "unknown lab" to testing a global vaccine. In what would normally take years, even decades to develop, Moderna produced one in only 2 months. I find that extremely strange.

Published on their website, Moderna admits the mRNA vaccine injects an "operating system" into your body that they call "The Software of Life."[7] Thus, the mRNA COVID vaccines are like a computer operating system, just like computer operating systems such as Gates' Windows, where there would be a "back door" where the Elite will be able to control our bodies through regular "updates."

Inside the COVID "shot" is something called hydrogel. Hydrogel is a technology invented by, oh guess who? DARPA.

Hydrogel contains microscopic nanobots which, when injected into you, not only modify your genes, but allow technology to interface with you.

In a nutshell, the "shot" allows you to be injected with genetic modification technology and nanobots that will permanently and irreversibly change your genetics…

Permanently and irreversibly!

Horrifyingly, by receiving this jab…knowingly or unknowingly… you've just voluntarily and irreversibly decided to join the Transhumanism movement!

And, lockstep with Transhumanism, Bill Gates and MIT

---

7. https://stateofthenation.co/?p=46766

developed the Human Implantable Quantum Dot Microneedle Vaccination Delivery System. The quantum-dot tattoos involve applying microneedles that contain the vaccine and fluorescent copper-based "quantum dots" embedded inside biocompatible, micron-scale capsules. During vaccine delivery the microneedles dissolve under the skin, leaving the encapsulated quantum dots. This invisible "tattoo" is made up of minuscule quantum dots which are tiny semiconducting crystals that reflect light and glow under infrared light. It's an inked tattoo which will include your identification Mark and vaccination records. The embedded ink tattoo is only visible using a special smartphone camera app and filter.

On-Demand Drug Delivery; brought to you by Bill Gates.

In other words, they've found a covert way not only to embed the record of a vaccination directly into a patient's skin rather than documenting it electronically, but also to track data 24/7. Who is in charge of collecting this real-time data? DARPA? Bill Gates? Why is the military involved in manipulating our genome with transfection?

The Bill and Melinda Gates Foundation funded the team's research, which was published in the journal *Science Translational Medicine*.[8] Gates announced on March 18, 2020, during a "*Reddit 'Ask Me Anything'* session" that he is working on the invisible Quantum Dot Tattoo Implant that will track who has been tested for COVID-19 and who has been vaccinated against it.

Bill Gates wants a "digital certificate" to show who has recovered from Covid-19 before they can fully move around in the marketplace. This ties into Bill Gates' *ID2020* which proposes a unique identifier. You won't need a driver's license, ID or credit card; you will just have this ID2020.

The Microneedle delivery technology, such as what Moderna is using, is designed after a viper fang. It is revealing, isn't it, that a

---

8. https://stm.sciencemag.org/content/11/523/eaay7162

deadly serpent (think Garden of Eden; Revelation 12:9) is used as a model?

The enzyme that will light up Bill Gates' Human Implantable Quantum Dot Microneedle Vaccination Delivery System says it all, it's called *Luciferase*.

Yes, you read that correctly, as in containing the word Lucifer.

Luciferase is a telling term for the class of oxidative enzymes that produce bioluminescence light. It is what makes the vaccination readable long after the victim has been injected. Essentially, we will be branded with an ID.

The name *Luciferase* was created and first used by Raphaël Dubois, a pharmacologist (as in *pharmakia*/sorcery, gee no surprise there). Dubois invented the words *luciferin* and *luciferase*, for the substrate and enzyme, respectively. Luciferases are widely used in biotechnology, for microscopy and as reporter genes for many of the same applications as fluorescent proteins. However, unlike fluorescent proteins, luciferase does not require an external light source.

Dr. Anthony Fauci has joined Gates in calling for some type of digital tracking system without which people will not be able to return to work or shop at their local grocery. High-tech companies like SuperCom have even produced scalable electronic monitoring and tracking platforms which they say are ready now to keep an eye on all, both small and great. And some countries have already passed legislation to make the coronavirus vaccine mandatory in vaccine passports, such as Canada's Prime Minister Trudeau.[9]

A June 6, 2021 press release outlined how a UN agency details specifications for a new "visible digital seal." UN's ICAO said, *"the seal stores datasets for 'test and vaccination certificates' in a two-dimensional* 'digitally-signed' *barcode which Border control and other*

---

9. https://www.ctvnews.ca/politics/vaccine-passports-to-be-expected-but-canada-not-ready-to-set-terms-yet-trudeau-1.5404349

receiving parties can verify the data against established requirements including through the use of traveler self-service kiosks and processes based on the same public key cryptographic infrastructure principles already used to support ePassport issuance and authentication by more than 145 countries globally."[10]

It is interesting to note that Klaus Schwab referred to unvaccinated people as "*a threat to humanity.*"[11] He and several dozen heads of the World Health Organization (WHO), the World Economic Forum (WEF), and various other globalist bodies have declared that the "Great Reset" needs to include the establishment of a "global pandemic treaty" to ensure that "all humans are vaccinated" in accordance with government edicts.[12]

On April 1, 2021, LA Times Columnist Harry Litman tweeted:

> "*Vaccine passports are a good idea. Among other things, it will single out the still large contingent of people who refuse vaccines, who will be foreclosed from doing a lot of things their peers can do. That should help break the resistance down.*"

He got 21,000 "likes." [13]

If the shadow cabal can use nanoparticles to edit your DNA for "good reasons," could they also use them to harm you? Before answering, think about all the nanoparticles in those delivery methods.

The answer is a resounding YES!

After all, they don't hide the fact that they want to reduce the population. Gates and other elites have long opined that there are too many people on the earth and something must be done. It is no

---

10. https://globalnews.ca/news/7936027/icao-vaccine-passports/
11. https://tapnewswire.com/2021/04/klaus-schwab-declares-unvaccinated-people-to-be-a-threat-to-humanity/
12. https://www.naturalnews.com/2021-04-05-globalist-klaus-schwab-declares-unvaccinated-people-threat.html
13. https://twitter.com/harrylitman/status/1376293633746366465?lang=en

coincidence that evil Gates gave a Ted Talk where he boasted vaccines can help cut global population by 10-15 percent.[14]

Yes, he said *cut* population. How does that work – by deactivating these vaccine-implanted operating systems in us? Apparently, Gates couldn't fix his Microsoft operating system to prevent endless computer viruses and updates, so why should we trust a man who wants to rid the population? And yet here he is, a computer programmer, not a scientist, spearheading a major step towards Transhumanism.

In addition to being the biggest private owner of farmland in the United States,[15] Gates also wants to literally block out the sun, using frightening geoengineering technology.

More hellish terraforming brought to you by the son of a top eugenicist. How coincidental…

An explosive study by researchers at the prestigious Salk Institute raised questions about the new vaccines that contain billions of spike proteins that could greatly increase the chances of severe illness or death.[16]

During a presentation (June 10, 2021, Steve Quayle's *Extinction Protocol* event), Dr. Sherri Tenpenny said:

> *"The main culprit is the spike protein. These spike proteins fuse to receptors on the surface of cells, allowing the virus' genetic code to invade the host cell, take over its machinery and replicate. If Covid-19 is primarily a vascular disease and if the main instrument of physical damage is the spike protein, then why are we injecting people with billions of spike proteins? Do you think it's a good idea to bypass the*

---

14. https://www.ted.com/talks/bill_gates_innovating_to_zero/transcript
15. https://www.theguardian.com/commentisfree/2021/apr/05/bill-gates-climate-crisis-farmland
16. https://www.salk.edu/news-release/the-novel-coronavirus-spike-protein-plays-additional-key-role-in-illness/

first (defense) of your immune system, and inject trillions of spike proteins in your cells?"

A "virus antidote" that turns people into hybrids. Brought to you by the global techno-hucksters. Wow.

Speaking of virus-caused hybrids, how about a virus that turns you into a human-animal chimera such as, well a deer for example.

Enter Sweet Tooth.

The Netflix movie Sweet Tooth chronicles a perilous adventure in a post-apocalyptic world, where a hybrid boy (half-human and half deer) searches for a new beginning with a gruff protector.

Hmmmm, a virus that creates hybrids . . . talk about predictive programming straight out of the pit of hell.

In the movie the virus is called the H5G9 virus.

Could that name stand for....

H = human

5G = fifth generation technology

9 = The Order of Nine Angels (O9A) a Satanic occult group, perhaps?

Also interesting is that of all the animals, the director happened to pick a Cernunnos/Pan style satyr-looking deer, like the centaur.

The very genetic code of humans and their home (the planet's biosphere) is being overwritten or as I call it terraformed. The ultimate goal is the ability to manipulate, patent and program at will the biological processes of all life.

The Globalists have become so bold, and the human masses have become so compliant, that they are no longer doing these things in secret, but are right out in the open for all to see. Hidden in plain sight. The world rolled over as the globalists yelled "roll up your sleeve!"

What Big Pharmakia Kingpins are doing by injecting gene

changing messenger RNA (mRNA) with nanobot technology components into people's bodies is transforming the human genome into something synthetic, rendering recipients as "non-human chimeras."

It appears as though we are now in the biggest human genome global mass "Dr. Mengele-style" experiment that ever hit planet earth. Have we unequivocally become lab rats to the global Elite? Even more frightening is, could a kill-switch have been installed to turn off/terminate the "new resulting human hybrid?"

In other words, if they are turning us into machines via the "vaxtech," then it stands to reason they can also shut down the machine. In other words, Insta-kill.

One question that I have is, looking at the staggering number of side effects and deaths from the vaccine at the time of this writing, are they already able to do that—trigger people's deaths?

Our genome is the very blueprint of what makes us us. The likeness and image of God is imprinted into our very DNA. As I said, The God Code.

Once we contain synthetic and synthesized genes and genomes, at what point do we become no longer human?

And a huge point is, if God offers salvation to humans only, what happens when you're not human? When we become an unsanctioned (not approved by God) chimeric hybrid entity, we are no longer human. Now that is a terrifying reality we are faced with.

As David Spangler said:

> "No one will enter the New World Order unless he takes a Luciferian initiation."[17]

In my opinion The COVID vaccine is that initiation.

They say soon 'no man will buy or sell' without the COVID Vaccine.

---
17. http://libertytree.ca/quotes_by/david+spangler

Marching towards the Mark of The Beast…

CHAPTER 10

TECHNOLON RISING: THE LAST STAND

"Finally, my brethren, be strong in the Lord, and in the power of his might. Put on the whole armor of God, that ye may be able to stand against the wiles of the devil. For we wrestle not against flesh and blood, but against principalities, against powers, against the rulers of the darkness of this world, against spiritual wickedness in high places. Wherefore take unto you the whole armor of God, that ye may be able to withstand in the evil day, and having done all, to stand. Stand therefore, having your loins girt about with truth, and having on the breastplate of righteousness; And your feet shod with the preparation of the gospel of peace; Above all, taking the shield of faith, wherewith ye shall be able to quench all the fiery darts of the wicked. And take the helmet of salvation, and the sword of the Spirit, which is the word of God: Praying always with all prayer and supplication in the Spirit." ~ Ephesians 6:10-18

Today we are being primed for the very same scenario that caused the destruction of mankind by the Great Flood. In the race to "Rebuild Babel," the cornucopia of emerging technoscience and genetic engineering, seething with demon-tech and Fallen Angel tech, promises to turn The Almighty's creation into Mutagenic Monsters and Hellish hybrids. We stand at the cusp of the Days of Noah 2.0.

We truly are in a 'Technological Babylon' …a *Technolon*.

Satanically-inspired mad scientists and Transhumanists would love to figure out the complexities of God's creation…our DNA, our brain, even our soul. Satan is the ultimate counterfeiter and he always plays the same deck of cards with no original thought of his own. He and his minions have always been intent on defacing mankind, created in God's own image because this would make God a liar. After all, He promised a hope and a future, that Jesus would never leave us or forsake us, and an eternity with Him in a new heavens and earth.

Fallen humans with limited intelligence are one thing, but a demon-possessed, beast-tech-style sentient super-intelligence that sees humans as mere pawns has the potential to lead humanity into an earth-based HELL.

And it won't stop there…

The growing digital monster will feed off our data stream and grasp for our life energies, in constant connectivity. Rewriting itself, growing, finding and fixing errors, with each iteration it will become more intelligent. And more dangerous.

This beast tech has the potential to become a monster of biblical proportions! Pun intended.

Remember it was in 2019 when Elon Musk said he planned on placing WiFi on the moon. Musk's SpaceX was poised to launch 60 satellites to space to provide InterNET service across the globe from a constellation of satellites whizzing around the planet. One might ask, is stringing out WiFi to the moon enabling a bigger push toward the powerful AI Beast System that will control the entire planet?

Talk about total coverage and immersion. Add to that a missile or other weapon platform using drones, autonomous vehicles, and robots, and it could potentially attack any nation on earth for full spectrum dominance and control.

The Beast broadcasting from the abyss of space to the bottomless pit. Imagine that.

When it comes to the ability of The Beast System to surveil the whole earth, it gives a whole new meaning to Satan being the prince of the power of the air. *Or maybe the airwaves?*

Obadiah 3, 4 says:

> "The pride of thine heart hath deceived thee (…) Though thou exalt thyself as the eagle, and though thou set thy nest among the stars, thence will I bring thee down, saith the Lord."

On the issue of connectivity, the already-booming internet of things (IoT) can expect a big boost when 6G (Genesis 6, anyone?) rolls out.

There has been a huge push to implement a global *techno-sorcery* ley line network across the planet to beam techno-frequency signals across the entire earth. This could also easily be used for a mass mind-control scenario like *Project Blue Beam*.

The 1938 CBS radio broadcast of Orson Welles' dramatization of *War of the Worlds,* a novel written 40 years earlier by H. G. Wells, created panic across the United States as millions of people tuned in and believed that earth was experiencing a *real* invasion by the Martians.[1] The broadcast was partially funded by the Rockefeller Foundation and guided by the Council on Foreign Relations, in what was later discovered to be a psychological operation (psyop, for short) to "test" panic and hysteria throughout the United States.[2]

---

1. Cantril, H. (1940). *The invasion from Mars: a study in the psychology of panic; with the complete script of the famous Orson Welles broadcast.* Princeton University Press.
2. The Engineering of Consent: Controlling Mankind's Past to Control Its Future by David Klooz, 2021.

Astonishingly, it was said to be heard by over six million people.

In Harlem excited crowds shouted that President Roosevelt's voice had warned them to "pack up and move north because the machines are coming from Mars."[3]

Dr. Hadley Cantril wrote a paper entitled, "The Invasion From Mars-A Study in the Psychology of Panic." Cantril's study examined the power of the radio broadcast media and its effects upon a population under the direct influence of fear.[4]

For years there have been rumors about a "Project Blue Beam" that was conducted by a secret government organization. This first became public in 1994 when journalist Serge Monast published his book, *Project Blue Beam*.[5]

According to Monast's research, during Project Blue Beam, which was developed by NASA, images would be projected onto a "screen" into the atmosphere. These images would appear at various vantage points on Earth. "Artificial thoughts" were also created which would cause people to "hear" messages/voices in their head as well as to "see" a programmed "event" occurring in real time. To do this, they used advanced holographic technology and EMF waves. These projected visual "hallucinations" could easily simulate a cataclysmic event such as an alien invasion or a second coming of Jesus scenario, or even a fake "rapture-type" event, thus laying the groundwork for a figure to appear, such as the biblical Antichrist.

It happened 8 decades ago with audio only, no visual. Think of the potential implications of people across the world experiencing mass psychological breakdowns and post-traumatic stress syndrome, as reality unravels around them.

---

3. https://www.nydailynews.com/news/national/war-worlds-broadcast-caos-1938-article-1.2406951
4. Cantril, H., pp 171-172.

5. Serge Monast, "Project Blue Beam, www.educate-yourself.org, 1994.

Remember in the beginning I talked about the return of these ancient god-men coming back to earth? With an expansive 5G/6G network across the planet, combined with the vast network of The Beast, this very scenario could absolutely happen.

"Even the very elect could be deceived," (if it were possible).

Speaking of surveying the stratosphere, I would like to point out that globalist Bill Gates, who as I've established has a penchant for depopulating the earth, announced plans to surveil the entire planet from space. Gates, who has his dirty hands in all things terrifying, is a significant player in a start-up company called EarthNow, which provides satellite imagery and live video in near real time. Through a new network of satellites, which is heavily dependent on AI, the company will be able to see any and every corner of the globe and provide live, real-time video (with only a second of latency).[6]

Talk about trying to be omnipresent!

Ye shall be as gods…

By now I am certain that a very insidious picture is starting to immerge. Our DNA is being transfected and used for data, digital avatars are becoming commonplace, and nanobots are being used for everything from "treating" diseases to spreading pathogens to making other robots. This technology is growing like a cancer, and it promises to completely reshape our world with the AI "gods" and their acolyte humans.

Techno overlords implementing Techno serfdom…

We can take a page out of Noah's book (literally), by seeing that he did not buy into the Transhumanist lies of his day. While the Watchers were promising advanced technology to the world in exchange for use of human DNA (1 Enoch 8), it must have been obvious to Noah how reminiscent this was of the serpent in the Garden who made similar beguiling promises of godlike abilities for

---

6. https://www.zdnet.com/article/backed-by-bill-gates-earthnow-wants-to-show-us-every-inch-of-our-planet-in-real-time/

those who partook of the forbidden fruit. Noah assumed leadership instead, independently maintaining his faith and focusing on God, not willing to compromise his flesh or that of his family for any temporal benefit.

Furthermore, Noah did not sit idly by, keeping his opinions to himself. In 2 Peter 2:5 we learn he became a preacher of righteousness, facing the Transhuman movement of his day with boldness, and warning of the dangers of grievous sin related to genetic corruption.

It is our duty as Believers to follow Noah's example and make known the manifold wisdom of God.

The fact that God's people could prevail over the spirit of the Nephilim in these ways is an ageless reality. It suggests that Believers today not only can survive, but can triumph over the inhuman threat represented by hellish technology. While it could certainly be possible to get discouraged by focusing on the prediction of their return at the end of the age, a wonderful portion of Scripture from the same Days of Noah adds:

"But Noah found grace in the eyes of the Lord."

Think about what a marvelous revelation this is! That at earth's darkest hour in history, when the sins of the Watchers had metastasized across continents and infected all of humanity.

"Noah walked with God."

At a time when all flesh was tainted and corrupted by transhuman genes and every imagination of men's thoughts were only evil continually, one man *walked with God;* one man found grace. Genesis 6

Today, as we move into the uncharted waters of a resurrected technological and human-transforming era, the keys to victory for Believers will be the same as they were for Noah, David, Joshua, Caleb, Paul, and many others (in both the Old and New Testament) —

knowing what to keep one's focus on, where to place one's faith, and whose champion we can be.

Jesus, addressing His disciples concerning the signs of His coming and of the end of the age, said it would be *as the Days of Noah were*, and *worse than it ever had been or ever would be again.* Matthew 24:21 and 37

This, friends, unveils good news, because while Nephilim were on earth during (and after) the antediluvian age, this was not the only sign related to ancient days. The Bible illustrates other signs too, having to do with God's covenant people (the remnant) and their unequaled ability through faith to turn back the Nephilim plans.

Consider how King Saul in 1063 BC stared across his tent into the eyes of the unproven youngest son of Jesse. By Providence, the teenager, David, had come on a mission for his father to deliver food and gather information regarding the welfare of his brothers. 1 Samuel 17 tells us that upon his arrival, Goliath, the Mighty Philistine Champion, stood up at his camp across the Valley of Elah and once again challenged the armies of Israel to send a warrior out against him. Two times a day for forty days the fearsome giant terrified Saul's army, crying out in a loud voice over the steep basin to the ranks of Israel:

> "Why are ye come out to set your battle in array? am not I a Philistine, and ye servants to Saul? choose you a man for you, and let him come down to me. If he be able to fight with me, and to kill me, then will we be your servants: but if I prevail against him, and kill him, then shall ye be our servants, and serve us. I defy the armies of Israel this day; give me a man, that we may fight together."

Saul and company, after hearing Goliath's taunt, became greatly afraid. On witnessing this spectacle, David's response was one of dismay at the lack of Israel's faith.

> *Who is this uncircumcised Philistine, that he should defy the armies of the living God?*

David shocked everybody with his direct retort to Goliath.

> *"You come at me with a sword and a shield, but I am coming in the name of the Lord of Hosts, the God of the armies of Israel, whom you have defied!"*

With that, David rushed forward, let the stone go from his sling, and the rest, as they say, is history.

Why is this story important? Because Goliath was a Nephilim, and he was defeated by a young servant of God. If the arrival of these beings or the spirit of their sins is the preeminent sign of the end times, David defeating one is germane, as well. The Bible says that no man knows the day or the hour that the Lord will return, but we are encouraged to look for the signs of the End of the Age, and not to fear.

> *For God has not given us the spirit of fear, but of power, of love, and of a sound mind. 2 Timothy 1:7*

True Believers are the salt of the earth and the only influence identified in Scripture as the power against which the gates of hell cannot prevail.

Transhumanists want immortality and to live forever but only God, through His Son, Jesus, promises actual eternal life. God will provide a new body, not fashioned like a cyborg, but one like the resurrected body of Jesus Christ. God promises all Believers the assurance of eternal life with Him. We have a Redeemer Who doesn't only promise eternal life, but will also deliver on His promise.

Unlike the Matrix-style "hatchery" in Aldous Huxley's *Brave New World*, you were formed and knit together in your mother's womb. You are *fearfully and wonderfully made*. God's hands *fashioned and made you* and *He knew you even before He formed you in the womb. Before you were born He consecrated you.* Psalm 139

Wow!

As a father has compassion on his children, so the Lord has compassion on those who fear Him; for He knows how we are formed, He remembers that *we are dust*. Our Lord is a loving Father, the Prince of Peace, Who wants only the best for each of us. If we put our trust in Him, He will renew our youth like the eagle, allowing us to soar in new, glorified bodies that will live eternally!

Jesus is the only One Who can grant eternal life. But that can't happen to those who have forsaken the Lord to join with those promising eternal life through DNA modifications or technological replacements for the human body. These mockers of eternal life are doomed to eternal damnation. The way that seems right to those worshiping at the feet of Post Humanism ends in death and punishment.

> *"Thinking themselves wise, they became fools." Romans 1:22*

Even though our culture is racing toward terrible things, God has shown us that, in the end, we win! For those who have placed their hope in God, there will be a loving Father to lead us into the Promised Land of Heaven. Jesus said:

> *I am the way, the truth, and the life: no man cometh unto the Father, but by me. John 14:6*

Undoubtedly there will be some of you reading this book who do not know Jesus Christ as your Lord and Savior. (Or maybe you've backslidden in your faith.) Fortunately, each human being has been blessed with free will and the choice is yours to make. Each of us can follow those who are busy pursuing a false hope of a limited "eternity" through man-made life-extension and the destruction of what it is to be human, or we can follow the genuine Redeemer.

The Lord wants human beings to remain pure, to separate themselves from these sinful things. The Lord wants His people to leave the sinful world, the culture of seduction.

Revelation 18:4-8 states:

> *"Then I heard another voice from heaven say: 'Come out of her, my people, so that you will not share in her sins, so that you will not receive any of her plagues; for her sins are piled up to heaven, and God has remembered her crimes.'"*

All that's necessary is that you admit that you have been sinful, repent (turn from) your sins, and pray to Jesus asking His forgiveness. You can do this in your own words or by using this simple prayer:

> *Lord Jesus,*
>
> *I'm a sinner and I've done a lot of things wrong in my life. I am sorry for these sins and ask that You forgive me. I believe that You, Jesus, as the only begotten Son of God, shed Your blood on the Cross, dying in my place because of my sins and that You paid my "tab" in full. I believe that You were raised from the dead and now sit at the right hand of The Father.*
>
> *Thank you, Jesus for saving me from my sins. I ask now that You'll lead me in the way I should go, and transform my life so that I can honor You in all I do.*
>
> *Thank you, Lord Jesus, for saving me from death and giving me eternal life.*
>
> *Amen.*

After you accept the Lord as your Savior, be sure to start reading the Bible. Good places to start are with the Gospels (Matthew, Mark, Luke and John) and Ephesians in the New Testament and the Psalms in the Old Testament.

Know that once you've made Jesus the Lord of your life, even though men may kill your body or you die of old age, your spirit will remain alive with Jesus. And one day He will resurrect your body into its incorruptible eternal form. And soon, Jesus will be rewarding those who remain close to Him with the words from Matthew 25:21:

> *"Well done, good and faithful servant!"*

It's my hope that you will choose the path of life through our Redeemer. I also hope you'll pass this book along to others so they may learn the truth as well. Much hangs in the balance, and your actions may very well determine where a friend or loved one will spend eternity.

> *"But he that shall endure to the end, the same shall be saved." ~ Jesus, Matthew 24:13*

Praise the Lord!

AFTERWORD

By now you can see that there has never been a time in history when prayer and targeted spiritual warfare is so urgently needed. As the end days fast approach, never before have we witnessed such a callous disregard for God and prayer. It is treated as a side note and a last resort, all while seducing spirits and false doctrines of devils abound. Ubiquitous debauchery and abhorrent sin are the order of the day as the church has become weak and anemic, too often nothing more than glorified social clubs with very little power.

The greatest tragedy facing modern Believers is how the church is disregarding, ignoring, and/or denying the power of the demonic realm. Defeating supernatural powers of the forces of darkness requires supernaturally-empowered Believers. The only way to stand against the wiles of the enemy is to be armed with the Word of God and to know how to use tactical warfare.

Satan has been operating undetected and unhindered by the saints of God for far too long. It's time for the church to begin to operate in the power and authority that Jesus shed His blood for, to do as He did to destroy the works of the enemy! (See 1 John 3:8.) We have superior weaponry, equipment, and power but unfortunately most Believers are woefully ignorant and living far beneath their birthright and their inheritance from God.

As we crash headlong into the beginnings of the terrible tides of wickedness sweeping the world, religious clichés and formulas will not work against our enemy. In the days ahead, the ability to lay hold of the power of God may easily determine the difference between life and death. Those unaware of or who deny the power of the demonic realm shall be helpless in the face of the coming all-out assault from the spirit world.

The power of the Living God is activated by prayer in the Name of Jesus Christ and is one of our biggest weapons against the enemy and the demonic hosts of hell.

It is vitally important for us to know the difference between prayer and warfare.

Prayer is addressing God; warfare is addressing the enemy.

You cannot leave out the part where you are addressing the enemy.

In Exodus 14:16, God told Moses to use the rod of authority that He had given him! It is time we take our rod of authority and take back ground for the Kingdom of God. It is time we acted like the soldiers of Jesus Christ that we are. We are in a spiritual battle. A soldier doesn't win a fight by hiding in defensive mode. No war was ever fought and won like that. It is time we started warring against the real enemy. Yes, our fight is a spiritual one! We cannot see into the spiritual realm, but it is every bit as real—if not more real—than what you see in front of you.

> *We are not fighting flesh and blood but against principalities, against powers, against the rulers of the darkness of this world, against spiritual wickedness in high places. Ephesians 6:12*

As soldiers in the army of the Lord, we need to understand that the weapons of our warfare are not carnal, but mighty through God to the pulling down of strong holds. It is time that we as Believers stopped living in ignorance, apathy, frustration, hopelessness, defeat, and bondage. It is an affront to what Jesus did on the Cross. It is time to use the power and authority that God has given you through His Son Jesus Christ!

Here are just a few examples from the Word of God:

> *James 5:16 "The effectual fervent prayer of a righteous man availeth much."*

Psalm 60:12 "Through God we shall do valiantly: for he it is that shall tread down our enemies."

Matthew 21:22 "Whatsoever ye shall ask in prayer, believing, ye shall receive."

Mark 11:24 "Therefore I say unto you, what things so-ever ye desire, when ye pray, believe that ye receive them, and ye shall have them."

Psalm 107:28 "Then they cry unto the Lord in their trouble, and he bringeth them out of their distresses."

Mark 9:29 "And he said unto them, This kind can come forth by nothing, but by prayer and fasting."

Ephesians 6:18 "Praying always with all prayer and supplication in the Spirit and watching thereunto with all perseverance and supplication for all saints."

Philippians 4:6-7 "Be careful for nothing; but in everything by prayer and supplication with thanksgiving let your requests be made known unto God. And the peace of God, which passeth all understanding, shall keep your hearts and minds through Christ Jesus."

Luke 10:19 "Behold, I give unto you power to tread on serpents and scorpions, and over all the power of the enemy: and nothing shall by any means hurt you."

Matthew 17:20 "And Jesus said unto them, for verily I say unto you, if ye have faith as a grain of mustard seed, ye shall say unto this mountain, remove hence to yonder place; and it shall remove; and nothing shall be impossible unto you."

Amen!

APPENDIX 1

WARFARE PRAYER AGAINST TECHNO-SORCERY, DIGITAL DICTATORSHIP & HUMAN EXTINCTION

Father in heaven, we come to You in the Name of Jesus Christ. We repent for our sins. We also repent for and renounce all whoredoms and idolatries off of each of us and our generational family lines. We close all doors and break all curses on our lives stemming from this iniquity.

Lord, You have given us all power over the enemy (Luke 10:19) and we exercise that power now.

Satan, we bind you, rebuke you, and render you powerless in Jesus' mighty Name.

We bind the strongman over our cities and our nation (Matthew 12:29). We bind in everlasting chains all principalities, powers, dominions, every wicked spirit, evil angel, familiar spirit, ancestral spirit, unclean spirit, worker of iniquity, soul hunter, soul scalper, witch, wizard, witch-doctor, sorcerer, necromancer, and all operators of evil.

We put the blood of Jesus Christ against all rituals, incantations, hexes, vexes, hoodoo, voodoo, Hinn and Jinn, magic, Juju, spells, spoken curses, chi, prana, aura, charm, and any object used by workers of iniquity against us, including astral projection.

We loose the judgment of God on every demonic entity that guards gates and portals, enforces walls, and forms weapons; we bind you, break your power and command you to go to the feet of Jesus Christ to be tormented before your time.

In the Name of Jesus, we sever every nefarious
transmission from satellites.

We come against all mind binding, witchcraft mind-control,
and demonic programming. We bind and break
the power of all constellation spirits of Arcturus, Mazzaroth,
Taurus, Mars, Betelgeuse and Marticus in Jesus' Name.
We bind up the prince of the power of the air
and all world ruler spirits in operation.

God, You said, no weapon formed against us shall prosper
(Isaiah 54:17), not even tech weaponry.

We take authority over all man-made
weapon or bioweapon systems, including 5G, EMF,
radiation, pulsed microwave, electromagnetic, psychotronic, sonic,
laser, frequencies, Scalar Waves, directed energy,
mind-control and manipulation.

We bind up all spirits operating through AI, nanotech, robots,
genetic engineering including CRISPR, and all technology,
all electronic devices, computers, iPads, mobile phones, fitness
trackers, etc. We command all Boyce, Boice and Bose
demons to go now in Jesus' Name.

We speak death to all heinous aerosols,
chemtrails (BAAL = Barium and Aluminum, etc.) and all
geoengineering.

We curse at the root all concoctions from the
pit of hell, causing us harm and command them to
dissolve and die now in Jesus' mighty Name!

We ask that all hidden documents, covenants,
contracts, agreements, certificates, oaths, and vows
be broken by the blood of Jesus.

We loose the mighty warring angels of God (Hebrews 1:14) with hammers (Zechariah 1:21) to smash the supply lines.

We send the curses back upon every transmitter. We ask you, Jesus, to send the wall of fire of the Holy Spirit (Zechariah 2:5) and burn the banners and scrolls of the enemy carrying out attacks against us.

We command division in the enemy camp.

We declare unrelenting judgment against the entire globalist agenda including the United Nations, DOD, DARPA, the vast network of sinister labs, universities, private defense contractors, pharmaceutical (pharmakia) companies, and any and all agencies complicit in these hellish attacks on God's people. We fall out of agreement with the enemy in this entire human extinction agenda and we ask You, Lord, to blot out and cancel every assignment against us.

We loose the judgment of Almighty God on these devils!

Father God, I ask forgiveness for and I speak supernatural reversal and neutralization to any and all damage done to me through any beast tech, demon tech, vaccine, shot, inoculation, (this includes if you received the covid jab), the cutting of my flesh or any foreign substance in my body.

I ask the Blood of Jesus to cleanse my DNA and every cell in every part of my body.

I speak supernatural healing to every system in my body (cardiovascular, digestive, endocrine, exocrine, immune, lymphatic, musculoskeletal, nervous, renal, respiratory, reproductive and sexual).

Father God, I now receive Holy Spirit's life-giving regeneration and renewal, in the Name of Jesus Christ.

We are Your people, and we ask You to send Your angels to tear up, root out and destroy every invisible barrier against us.

We decree that You alone are our shield, buckler, rearguard, strong tower, and fortress. We ask for Your divine protection and we put our trust and faith in You.

We give You all praise, honor and glory, and we ask this in the mighty Name of our Lord and Savior, Jesus Christ.

Amen and Amen.

Made in the USA
Middletown, DE
14 September 2021